You Can't Play Outside...

You Can't Play Outside...

By

Priscilla Sullins & Connie Baker

© 2002 by Priscilla Sullins and Connie Baker. All rights reserved.

No part of this book may be reproduced, stored in a retrieval system, or transmitted by any means, electronic, mechanical, photocopying, recording, or otherwise, without written permission from the author.

ISBN: 1-4033-7240-3 (e-book)
ISBN: 1-4033-7241-1 (Paperback)
ISBN: 1-4033-7242-X (Hardcover)

Library of Congress Control Number: 2002094265

This book is printed on acid free paper.

Printed in the United States of America
Bloomington, IN

1stBooks - rev. 11/07/02

For Patsy

AUTHORS' NOTE

The tragic crime in this book occurred in 1955, over forty-five years ago. In addition to numerous interviews, we researched newspapers, magazines and court documents to gather information. However, most of the people who played major roles in this incident are deceased. This includes both detectives, most policemen, one of the defense attorneys and many family members of both parties. Unfortunately, all family members of Patricia Ann Cook and Willie Grady Cochran, that we were able to contact, were unwilling to speak with us. We were able to interview one of the defense attorneys, a former ATF agent, a former police officer, neighbors, and acquaintances of both parties.

We created the entire text that appears in italics at the beginning of this book. Without input from family members, we devised the conversations in Chapters Four through Seven on the foundation of actual events. We created these from our extensive research and they are our interpretations of what seemed reasonable, based on that research.

All the testimony that appears in quotations in the trial chapters are taken directly from the Evidence Record at the Bartow County Courthouse. Errors in grammar, spelling and punctuation were not corrected, but left intact, as we felt it evoked the atmosphere and speech of that time.

The following names are fictitious, but represent real people: Jake Carson, Mary Carson, Evelyn Johnson, Mr. and Mrs. H. H. Duncan, Harris Cochran, George Fowler, Myrtle Scoggins, Jane Kinsey, Lillian Dempsey, Henry Smith, and Nancy Jones.

PROLOGUE

"You can't play outside; I don't have time to watch you." This was a refrain heard by children in North Georgia in 1955 and for years afterward.

1955. Eisenhower was president, Disneyland opened, and Crest toothpaste was introduced. It was the year that children lined up to receive the newly developed Salk polio vaccine. The vaccine was administered by injection - sugar cubes were years in the future.

Before 1955, children were encouraged to play outside. They played with friends, rode bikes through the neighborhood and walked to the store without fear. The summer of 1955 changed that forever. For the children, that summer was a defining moment.

We were those children.

In November 2001, we read an obituary in a local newspaper that stated the deceased was preceded in death by a sister, Patricia Ann Cook. More than forty-five years had passed, but the memories of childhood dread and fear were still fresh.

We had been told about a child being kidnapped from her backyard. We learned the definition of "dragging the river." Unsupervised play had become a thing of the past. Evil had become a reality.

Our lives were changed that summer and we will always remember why.

Monday morning, June 20th, 1955. In north Georgia it was not yet officially summer, but the days were getting hot. Early that morning, around six thirty, the temperature was still in the fifties as Willie Grady Cochran left Paulding County, Georgia headed north to Rome. It would take almost an hour. He was going to visit his brother who was incarcerated at the Floyd County Public Works Camp for a minor alcohol related offense.

He arrived at the prison camp around eight thirty. He drove around behind the prison facility to the warden's house. Driving into the yard, he noticed the small, white house had a wide front porch that looked shady and cool. As he stepped out of the truck and started toward the house he saw flowers planted along the walk. When he knocked on the door, a pretty, young girl answered.

"Can I help you?" she asked.

"I'm looking for Warden Caldwell. I need to see my brother to sign some papers so I can use his truck," Willie Grady replied.

"The Warden's my daddy, but he won't be back for 'bout half an hour."

Willie Grady stared. The teenager was pretty, dressed in shorts and a T-shirt. Willie Grady realized he should say something, but couldn't think what as he looked at her. The girl looked back, waiting for him to answer. Maybe she saw something in his eyes, maybe she just thought he was ill-mannered. She was glad the screen door was locked. She and her sister had been taught from an early age to keep the doors locked because of the close proximity to the prison. She shut the wooden door and, after a moment's hesitation, locked it. Willie Grady went back to his truck and wondered if anyone was in the house with the girl.

Suddenly a car pulled up to the front of the house.

"What you need here?" a big man in a wide brimmed hat called.

"I'm looking for my brother, Harris, Mr. Caldwell. I need him to sign these papers, so I can keep his truck 'til he can get out."

The warden looked him up and down. The man had nerve just showing up at his house. He didn't like it.

"Give me the papers. Get in your truck and follow me to the camp. I'll get a trusty to take them to your brother and see if he'll sign 'em."

An hour later, Willie Grady had the signed papers and was on his way to Milner Motor Company in Rome with the papers he needed to have the truck registered in his name.

He was feeling really fine now. He had a new Ford truck and some money in his pocket. He knew of a place nearby where he could buy a drink. He drove to Mable's. Mable had a house on East Fourteenth Street. He was familiar with it and he'd been there several times in the last week. The house sat on a corner and was surrounded by a chain link fence. You could buy alcohol and women at Mable's. Willie Grady pulled into the driveway and around to the back of the house. There was a screened porch and he knocked on the door. A young, black woman answered his knock. She was the cook and housekeeper.

"What you need, Mister?"

"Hey there Bobbie, I sure hope you have a few cold ones in there," replied Willie Grady.

He left with four cold beers, and although Bobbie couldn't say why, she was glad he left quickly.

It was now almost eleven o'clock. The temperature was rising and the humidity was beginning to thicken the air. Willie Grady drove his new truck and drank his cold beer. He was feeling better all the time, but that itchy, restless feeling was nagging him.

He had been out of prison over four months, and he had a regular job at the sawmill in Paulding County. He thought about buying himself a tractor-trailer rig. He'd had this plan for awhile now. He'd use the tractor-trailer to haul frozen poultry up North. Chicken houses were plentiful in north Georgia and he could make a good living being his own boss.

Willie Grady decided to drive to Lindale, a small community about eight miles out in the county. Once he got there he stopped at another bootlegger's place and had another beer. He drove to a local auto repair shop to talk to some friends.

Willie Grady told the owner, "I'm going to Rome to find a fella that owes me twenty dollars."

On the drive back to Rome, Willie Grady began to think about women. He remembered the girl at the Public Works Camp. He began to get a little dizzy. He'd had several beers and the day was getting hotter.

He stopped the truck on East Seventh Street. He looked across the street and saw a man coming out of a house carrying boxes to his car. Four girls followed him. They seemed to all be talking at once. Three of the girls looked like children, but one was older. The older girl was wearing white shorts and a striped shirt. The man and the girls made two more trips in and out of the house while Willie Grady watched from across the street. The man hugged all four girls and left in the car.

Willie Grady felt sweat roll down his back. He felt nervous, excited, expectant. He got out of the truck, crossed the street and walked to the front door. The screen door was closed but not the wooden one, and he could see into the house. The older girl must have heard him because she was standing there, right inside the screen door.

"I'm looking for a Miz Crawford who lives somewhere around here. She's a widow woman. Do you know her or where she lives?" Willie Grady asked the girl.

He looked at her legs and thought that she shouldn't wear her pants so short. It made it hard for him to concentrate.

The girl said, "I don't know anyone by that name, but my mama is next door. I'll just call out the window and maybe she'll know."

He watched her turn around and go out of the room. He was really sweating now. The humidity was high and he could hear a faint rumble of thunder. Suddenly she was back, right next to the screen.

"My mama doesn't know of anyone around here by that name, either."

Willie Grady didn't reply, just stood there on the porch and stared. Finally, he turned and stepped off the porch. Now the girl was nervous. The man was acting strangely and kept looking at her legs. Her mother was next door, but her sisters had gone to the library and she was alone in the house. She put the latch on the screen door and backed into the room, out of the man's sight. Willie Grady walked across the street to his truck and drove away.

As he turned onto East Eleventh Street, he saw a black woman waiting at the bus stop.

He pulled the truck over and leaned out the window. "Do you know where I can find a young girl to do some work for me?"

The woman hesitated, "Nossir, I don't know of nobody right now, but if you tell me your name and address, maybe I could see if I could find you somebody."

She thought he was drunk and she didn't want to talk to him, but she didn't want to make him mad either. She just wanted him to drive on. Willie Grady sat there. The new truck, his plans, the heat, the humidity, the beer, the girls in shorts, his desires. All these things swirled and churned in his mind. He really needed to find a girl. He didn't want to think why.

"You're sure you can't find me, uh, you don't know where I can find a young girl to work?" Willie Grady asked again.

"No sir, I don't, but if I had your name and address I could call you if I found somebody," she repeated.

"Thanks anyway," Willie Grady said as he drove towards East Nineteenth Street.

As he turned onto East Nineteenth Street, Willie Grady saw a young woman sweeping off her porch steps. He stopped his truck and walked into the yard.

"Do you know anyone, any family around here by the name of Crawford?" he asked the woman.

She held her broom still and said, "No, I surely don't, but my aunt's in the house lying down. I'll go ask her. She might know them."

The young woman turned and went into the house. She felt uneasy. She was glad she wasn't alone.

Willie Grady stood in the sun and heard another distant rumble of thunder. He considered that the woman's aunt was home. It was two o'clock.

"I asked my aunt, and she doesn't know any Crawfords," the woman, now on the porch again, said.

"Well, thanks anyways," he said as he got into his truck.

Willie Grady Cochran slowly drove down East Nineteenth Street. At number 618 he saw a white house, and in the backyard he saw a girl sunbathing in the heavy, wet, Georgia heat. She had short, blonde hair and was wearing a faded red swimsuit. A flowered robe lay beside her. Willie Grady Cochran stopped his truck.

Patricia Ann Cook, age fourteen, saw the truck stop and picked up her robe, hearing her mama's voice telling her never to answer the door in her bathing suit.

She had been to the dentist that day. Her stepmother had taken her and brought her back home. Her mother and stepfather were both at work. Patricia had called her mother when she returned home and told her that she would start supper later, but first she wanted to get some sun. It was hot and Patricia didn't have a way to go to the nearby pool, so she decided to just sunbathe awhile.

Ruby Waters had told her daughter, "Just don't stay out there too long. You might blister if you do."

Having a suntan was important for teenagers in the South in 1955. Skin cancer, sunscreen and the ozone layer were unknowns. Butter, cooking oil and the all-time favorite, a mixture of baby oil and iodine, were used to achieve a deep, dark tan. "Blistered" was a term used in the South, then and now, to denote serious sunburn.

Willie Grady walked through the front yard to the door and knocked. Patricia opened the door. She wore her bathing suit and her flowered robe. Willie Grady looked at her legs. He saw her blue eyes.

He would later tell a police officer, "She didn't look like no kid."

He said to her, "I'm looking for a family named Crawford, I think they live around here. Do you know them?"

"I don't know anyone by that name," Patricia replied. "My mother or stepfather might know them, but they're not here right now."

"Well, it looks like you're about to go to the pool," Willie Grady said.

He was really disturbed by the girl's attire. She had on a robe, but the image of her without it remained. He could see her bathing suit, her legs, her blonde hair, her blue eyes. Girls shouldn't dress like that.

Patricia had no experience with malevolence. It had not existed in her world of a loving and kind family. Cruelty had never shown its face in her life experience. She saw a thin, dark, attractive man. She wanted to be helpful. She was always friendly.

"No, I don't have a ride to go swimming. I'm just getting some sun here at home."

"I'd be happy to give you a ride to Roy's pool, won't take five minutes. It's right on my way."

He'd sure like to take her to the pool. He'd enjoy having her in the truck and being able to look at her, maybe touch her. He could tell she liked him because she was smiling and showing off her legs.

"That sounds good, but I can't leave the house, my mother would really be mad at me for that. I hope you find the Crawfords. Somebody else on the street might know them."

She began to back away to close the door.

It happened so fast. Willie Grady pulled the screen door open and gripped her arm. A gun was in his other hand.

"Oh yeah, we're going to the pool, sweetie."

They were on the porch.

Willie Grady looked at her and said, "Don't move."

He let go of her arm, but kept the gun low, near his waist, pointed at Patricia. He reached behind him and closed the door.

"Just walk to the truck, right there. Don't say anything and don't try to run. I'll shoot you if you do. We're just going to take a little ride and then I'll take you to Roy's. Move! Start walking."

Patricia was terrified. What was happening? How did she get on the porch? Where did the gun come from? What was the man saying? She couldn't get her breath. She knew she must do what he said or he'd shoot her.

Willie Grady walked behind Patricia. She could feel the gun against her back. He opened the passenger door of a light green truck. He pushed the gun hard into her side. She got in.

"Why are you doing this? You're really scaring me. Please, please, I don't want to go anywhere, please. What are you going to do?"

Patricia was crying. She tried to think of what to do. Her legs began to shake uncontrollably, then her whole body was shaking. She felt like she was going to be sick.

"Shut up. Just sit there. Be quiet, now."

Willie Grady got in the truck. He drove up East Nineteenth Street toward the pool. His hands began to shake. She looked so pretty. She shouldn't have been wearing that bathing suit. It wouldn't be his fault if something happened. He drove past Roy's pool and headed toward Bartow County. She was crying, getting louder, begging him to stop and let her out. He drove with one hand and pointed the gun at her.

"Shut up! Listen to me! You'd better be really quiet. If you don't hush right now, I'll shoot you here. If you be quiet, I won't hurt you."

Patricia was near hysteria. He was yelling at her. He punched her in the arm and in the ribs with the gun. She cried out, but she knew he would kill her if she didn't hush. She must do everything he said or he would hurt her. She bit her tongue to stop crying. She was so cold, she couldn't stop shivering. Patricia began to go into shock.

Willie Grady's throat was dry. He'd had several beers during the day and it was after three o'clock. He knew he needed to get out of town, out of the populated area. He drove to Chulio Road, a country road leading to Bartow County. He was familiar with that area and knew there were few houses there. Patricia was not saying anything now.

"I'm pretty thirsty, do you want something to drink?" he asked her.

She was sort of scrunched in the corner of the truck against the door. She looked at him with a blankness in her eyes but nodded her head.

"I'm going to stop at Duncan's store to get Cokes and if you know what's good for you, you'll keep your mouth shut."

He knew he was close to a store where he could get cold drinks at a "drive up." Duncan's was a small, one room, country store attached to the owner's residence. Willie Grady pulled the truck up and honked the horn. A man came to the door and Willie Grady told him to bring them two Double Colas.

Patricia saw a woman come out onto the porch. She noticed Willie Grady looking at the store. Furtively she raised her hand and motioned the woman toward her.

The woman saw her and called from the porch, "Do you need something?"

"He's waiting on us," Willie Grady said as the man brought the drinks to the car.

Patricia's hope for rescue faded as Willie Grady paid the man and quickly drove away.

Willie Grady tried to think where to take the girl. By now he knew what he was going to do. He drove and drank his Double Cola. He looked at Patricia and was both excited by her and angry at her. They were in an isolated area near Mullinax Mountain.

He stopped and pulled Patricia across the seat and out of the truck. He pulled her robe off and led her into the woods. Patricia was silent, terrified, tears streaming down her face.

Willie Grady knew of an old cabin in the woods, and he took her there. Once inside, he began to touch her.

It was hot and he was sweating. She smelled the alcohol. Terrified, she screamed.

"Shut up!" he told her.

But she couldn't, she was past hearing him. Terror and survival merged in her. Willie Grady realized that she was out of control and decided to take her to a place that he knew would be safer for him.

"Hush," he said, "I'm not goin' to hurt you. Come on, we'll get another Coke and I'll take you home."

He dragged her back to the truck.

He was still thirsty from the excitement, heat, and alcohol. He stopped at another country store, warning Patricia not to move or speak. She noticed a woman walking into the store and stared intently at her. It was all she could manage. He brought back two Double Colas for himself and a Coca-Cola for Patricia.

He remembered an old logging road he had traveled before. He drove to the Old Lucas Road and pulled the truck over. They were in an isolated, wooded area. Willie Grady got out of the truck, walked around to the passenger side and opened the door.

"Get out and let's take a walk."

Patricia's knees buckled when she stepped out. Her eyes were glassy and she did not speak, only making whimpering sounds. Willie Grady took her arm and led her further into the trees. He sat down beneath a large oak tree and pulled Patricia down beside him.

Willie Grady defiled the child's innocence and trust. He violated the laws of man and desecrated the laws of God. Willie Grady Cochran embraced evil.

When he had finished, Willie Grady was afraid. He was on parole and he did not want to return to prison. He told Patricia to lie still and went to the truck for his gun. He walked back to her and sat down.

Patricia looked at him and said, "What are you going to do?"

"Well, we can't both leave here. So I'm gonna have to shoot you."

She drew her knees up to her chest and turned on her side, away from him. Willie Grady put the gun to her back and pulled the trigger. Now Patricia Ann Cook would never tell anyone what he'd done.

He had assured her silence but there remained the problem of the body.

Willie Grady left her there in the woods. He covered her body with leaves, went to his truck and drove toward home. He went to another brother's house in Paulding County before dark, a little after seven in the evening. His brother and a friend were sitting on the porch.

Willie Grady went out to the fence and began to cut some baling wire that had been left there. His brother called out to him and asked him what he was doing.

"I'm just getting a piece of wire down here, I'll see you after a while."

He drove to his mother's house, went to a shed behind the house and hid the gun there. He found a large wrench and a heavy logging chain in the shed and took them along with a quilt from the house.

Willie Grady drove back to the Old Lucas Road and wrapped Patricia Ann's body in the quilt. He lapped the logging chain around the quilt and fastened the heavy wrench to the chain with the baling wire. He carried *her body to the truck and drove to a bridge over the Etowah River. He stopped the truck in the middle of the bridge and dropped the child's body into the river.*

Willie Grady drove home with the windows down. He was finally cooling off.

He was finished.

You Can't Play Outside...

CHAPTER 1

When Patricia Ann Cook's picture and the story of her disappearance appeared on the front page of the *Rome News Tribune,* Rome, Georgia was still a small town. Located in the northwest corner of Georgia, it was fifteen miles to Alabama and seventy miles to Tennessee.

Almost any tourist information about Rome, Georgia will include the phrase "nestled in the foothills of the Appalachian Mountains." Rome was founded in 1834 at the juncture of three rivers, the Etowah, the Oostanala and the Coosa. The city was originally settled around seven hills. The name was suggested because of the seven hills of Rome, Italy.

White settlers coming to the area in the late 1700's found the area populated by Cherokee Indians. This Cherokee tribe was quite civilized, having developed their own alphabet and published their own newspaper.

By the mid-1800's, river trade was bustling and a railroad was built. This was the time of "King Cotton" in the South. Many of Rome's citizens prospered by ginning and selling the white bolls.

In 1860 came the "War for States Rights." Several battles were fought in and around Rome. One story that has survived through the years is that of Rome's own "Paul Revere," John Wisdom. Wisdom, a former Roman whose mother still lived there, was a mail carrier and owned a ferry near Gadsden, Alabama. When Gadsden was attacked and burned by Union troops, he learned that they were headed for Rome. He left Gadsden on May 2, 1863, to warn the city. Stopping at farmhouses along the way to change horses, Wisdom made the sixty-five mile trip in eleven hours. He used five horses and one mule, and arrived at his mother's home in Rome by midnight. He was well ahead of the Federal troops, giving the city time to prepare.

In 1864, Rome was occupied for several months by Union troops, including General Sherman and his staff. When the troops pulled out, Sherman gave the order to burn everything that might be beneficial to the Confederates and much of Rome was burned. These were hard times for Georgia and the South. During Reconstruction, however, Rome rebounded and the Clock Tower, Rome's principal landmark, was erected in 1871.

Romans fought in both World Wars and in Korea. Their families buried sons, brothers, husbands and fathers in the now historic cemetery at Myrtle Hill.

In the early fifties, several businesses located in Rome. The General Electric Plant, Inland Container and Georgia Kraft Paper Mill were some of the industries that were supplied electricity by Plant Hammond in Rome, Georgia.

In 1955 the population of Rome was around thirty thousand. A small town atmosphere prevailed. To buy a really special dress, Romans went seventy miles south to Atlanta, Georgia, or about the same distance north to Chattanooga, Tennessee. The economy was up, and almost anyone could achieve the status of "middle class." The Baby Boomers were children. Boys wore crew cuts and girls wore poodle skirts. Most daddies worked and lots of mommies stayed home. Rome was the county seat of Floyd County, a "dry" county for wine and liquor where only beer could be purchased legally. "Spirits" were bought in Atlanta.

"Beer joints" were fairly common and several restaurants served beer, but not on Sunday.

Of course, there were always the bootleggers. Knowing where to go meant one could buy beer on Sunday. Most of these establishments were simply the homes of bootleggers, and bonded whiskey and moonshine were available.

At least two "houses of ill repute" were also located in Rome where alcohol, along with other pleasures, could be purchased. These establishments paid weekly "dues" to local law enforcement in order to operate freely, although discreetly. This was not an unusual arrangement in some places in the South in the 1950's.

Integration was not a real topic yet. Political correctness had not even been conceptualized, although it was proper to say Negro or colored instead of something more offensive. "Black" was yet to become beautiful in the future sixty's. Most public facilities were segregated. Change was on the way, however. In 1955, in Alabama, Rosa Parks refused to give up her seat on the bus to a white man.

Physical and mental disabilities were not treated sensitively either. People had nicknames like "Bad Eye" Culberson. The state mental hospital in Milledgeville, Georgia was for lunatics.

Summer in Georgia is hot and humid. It begins in May and ends in September. In the 1950's, there was no such thing as central air conditioning. Some houses had attic fans to pull a breeze through, though the air would be warm. Windows and doors were left open twenty-four hours a day. Many people did not even own keys to their homes.

The big meal of the day was called dinner and was served at midday. The evening meal was called supper. "Dinner" was usually started in the morning, soon after the breakfast dishes were cleared, to avoid having the stove on during the hottest part of the day. The leftovers from dinner would be served for supper. This meant that the morning hours were usually busy for the woman of the house. Children were sent outside to play so as not to be underfoot.

In most neighborhoods there were several children of the same age group who played together. There were no such things as video games and computers. Those were the stuff of which science fiction was made. After all, television was still relatively new. All television programs were in black and white and there were no remote controls. Rooftop antennae provided access to Atlanta and Chattanooga stations. The most popular programs that year were "I Love Lucy," "The Honeymooners," and westerns such as "The Lone Ranger" and "The Roy Rogers Show." No one had ever heard the term, "couch potato."

Summer days were spent riding bicycles and roaming through entire neighborhoods with friends. Mothers often didn't see their children until time for a meal. Youngsters who lived in rural areas frequently camped out. They set up their campsites in wooded areas, near their homes, and would stay for two or three days. No one, parents or children, ever thought of danger.

Another favorite pastime on those hot, summer days in Georgia, was swimming. Sometimes, playmates simply splashed around in small, plastic wading pools in a backyard. It was only about ankle-deep, but it helped beat the heat. Other times, simple games involved running through the spray of a garden hose. A trip to one of the local pools was, however, the ideal.

There were two public pools (for whites) in Rome: the Rome City Pool, managed by the city, and Roy's, (a public, for profit enterprise) owned by a local businessman.

The City Pool was surrounded by a fence and had a lifeguard, so it was not unusual for mothers to drop off their children for an afternoon and return at an appointed time to take them home.

Roy's was another story. There was no lifeguard. It was a "swim at your own risk" proposition. In addition, there was no fenced-in enclosure. Roy's Little Garden was a multi-faceted business, the swimming pool, a small grocery store, and a restaurant. Atop the restaurant, there was a glass enclosure where a local radio station aired "The Talk of the Town," a popular music show. Rock and roll music could be heard all around the pool as teens listened to their transistor radios. This was a favorite "hangout" for teenagers. Younger children weren't taken to Roy's pool unless a parent had the time to stay with them.

Another favorite teenage hangout was Turkey Mountain Lake, located in the north end of the county. It was a recreation center which included a lake, a swimming pool, a miniature golf course and a roller skating rink.

There were also two pools in southern Floyd County, Cave Spring Pool and Winwood Pool. Winwood was privately owned and, in addition to the pool, there was a lake with rowboats, where one could fish or float idly for relaxation. It was located on Cave Spring Road.

The Cave Spring Pool was, and still is, located in Cave Spring, Georgia, home of Georgia School for the Deaf. The pool, located in a beautiful setting with a large tree-shaded picnic area, also held other delights. In addition to the spring, which fed the pool and made the water icy, there was a large cave close by to explore. Visits to this pool usually involved spending the day.

Of these four pools, only Cave Spring is still open today. The City Pool was filled in and tennis courts built. Winwood is now private property, and all that is left of Roy's Little Garden is the store. The remnants of the restaurant and radio station stand empty and the pool is a gaping hole in the ground. There is no hint of its former glory.

Besides the above-mentioned public pools, there were private pools to enjoy. There were two country clubs at that time in Rome. Coosa Country Club, located next to the Coosa River, was near downtown Rome. This was where the "upper crust" of Rome society were members. These were the doctors, the lawyers, the local businessmen, and "old Rome money." There was (and still is) a pool, a golf course, and a restaurant in the clubhouse, where society and business luncheons were held and where members could dine.

Callier Springs Country Club had a predominantly middle class membership. It was on the outskirts of town and boasted a pool, golf course, and a clubhouse.

Another private pool was the Celanese Pool. It was owned by the Celanese Corporation, a textile manufacturer, for the exclusive use of its employees and their families.

Any of these private pools could be enjoyed if you were fortunate enough to have a friend whose family had a membership and would take you as a guest.

The City of Rome sponsored a local Teen Club on Friday nights. It was held at the Civic Center and was a gathering place for teenagers to dance and socialize. At the Teen Club there were no live bands, only someone playing 45 rpm's on a hi-fi record player. The era of Rock and Roll was just beginning. That year teens danced to "Rock Around the Clock" by Bill Haley and the Comets, and "Maybelline" by Chuck Berry. Elvis was a regional star, not yet nationally known.

Another favorite pastime in those days was going to the movies, or "going to the show," as it was called. There were two options - going to a "walk-in" at the downtown movie theaters, or going to a drive-in. The "walk-ins" included the Gordon, which closed in the 1960's, and in whose building there is now a local restaurant; the First Avenue, subsequently torn down and whose area is now a part of Southeastern Mills, a local manufacturer of flour; and the Desoto, now owned by Rome Little Theater and still used as a theater for plays. All of these were fairly large, each of which had a stage, a balcony, and an ornately designed interior. These theaters were also "white only." The Carver was the theater for blacks and was located on East Fourteenth Street. It later became a nightclub known as The Flamingo Lounge. All of Rome's white theaters were owned by one local family. The Carver was owned by a local black businessman.

"Going to the show" was an inexpensive diversion. In the mid-1950's, the admission price for adults was 35 cents and 15 cents for children under the age of twelve. At the snack bar a Coke or a candy bar cost a nickel and a box of popcorn was a dime.

Popular movies in 1955 were "The Seven Year Itch" with Marilyn Monroe, "East of Eden" and "Rebel Without a Cause" starring James Dean (who would be killed in a car accident that year), and Disney's "The Lady and the Tramp."

Drive-in movies were great, too. Cars were loaded with family, friends and even the dog, if you were so inclined. There was usually a playground under the giant screen with swings and seesaws for the children to play on if they got bored with the movie. Nobody worried. It didn't matter that it was dark and the children couldn't be seen. They would come running back to the car when the movie was over. It never occurred to anyone that they wouldn't, not until 1955.

The city school for whites was Rome High School and Negroes went to Main High. There were seven other white high schools for Floyd County residents, and a private prep school for boys.

It was a segregated society in those days. The predominant black social and business district was at Five Points, so named because it was at the juncture of five city streets. In an area of approximately a quarter mile were churches, barber shops, a pharmacy, a doctor's office, an insurance company, a black Masonic Hall, a grocery store with a cafe and the social center, the Spider Web Cafe. All these establishments were owned by local black businessmen. The Spider Web boasted a blue, neon spider web sign and was the meeting place for the community. Black teenagers gathered there after school for ice cream and conversation.

All in all, it was a nice place to live; not too big like Atlanta, and not too small to be boring. People were friendly and knew their neighbors. If someone had a death in the family, neighbors brought food to the house and took up money in the neighborhood for a floral arrangement. Kids played outside after dark.

It was a paradox...

Where there was wholesomeness, there was also corruption. Society in the 1950's was compartmentalized. Law enforcement protected society. However, in order to control the criminal element, the law became part of it to some degree. There was a dialogue between law enforcement and the criminal element that was allowed to flourish. Certain establishments were sanctioned for a price, allowing law enforcement to control them. Because of this relationship, competitive criminal elements were not allowed. People felt safe because crime was in its place (compartment). Bad things happened, even murders. but they were not random and therefore, not frightening. Venturing into unsavory compartments could be risky. Staying in the wholesome compartment assured safety. This was the stage on which the events of June 1955 were played in Rome, Georgia.

The compartmentalized society was shocked, sickened and outraged at the kidnapping, rape and murder of Patricia Ann Cook. Something terrible had happened to an innocent. She had not been in the wrong place. She had been at home. She should have been safe. Some sacred rule had been broken and justice would be swift and certain.

CHAPTER 2

Willie Grady Cochran was born on October 2, 1918, in Paulding County, Georgia, the fifth of seven children. He had four brothers and two sisters. He came from a good family, good in the sense of honest, hard working, and respected.

Willie Grady, as he was called, (this being very common in the South of that time, to call children by both their given names) grew up poor in a rural community called Burnt Hickory, just a few miles from the Bartow County line. Poverty, however, was not an unusual circumstance for the families in the rural South during his formative and teen years of the 1920's and 1930's. In the 1930's, during the Great Depression, the entire nation was struggling with poverty. Being poor at this time would certainly not have set him apart from his peers.

Willie Grady's father owned a cotton seed house. He was said to have been a heavy drinker who spent a period of time in the state mental hospital at Milledgeville, Georgia for an unspecified psychosis. Cochran felt that his father had been mean to him throughout his life and, in later years, would remember him as being drunk a lot and beating him. In point of fact, he had no pleasant memories of his father who had died in a cotton seed house fire in January, 1934, when Willie Grady was sixteen years old.

Warmth and affection were not emotions evoked by memories of either of his parents. Though a feeling of hostility toward his mother was also evident, there was still a bond of sorts with her. He stated that he got along well with her as long as she did not nag him.

Nothing much is known of Cochran's early life in Paulding County, other than he left school in the sixth grade. Later a psychiatrist would determine that he was "close to average" intelligence. He is remembered by one of his defense attorneys, Jere White, as being "well spoken," with a good vocabulary. Though there was mention of some sort of birth injury, there was apparently no physical or mental manifestation of it. It would appear, however, that his family might have used this as an excuse for his deviant behavior as he was growing up.

Willie Grady's school years were marred by a lack of socialization skills. He was unable to relate or interact favorably with teachers or students, and rarely participated in group activities. A family friend stated that he was always a problem for his parents, that he would run away from home, that he got into trouble a lot and that he could never hold a job. In fact, he seemed to be incorrigible.

This might explain his perception of his relationship with his parents. When Willie Grady was growing up, parents were much stronger disciplinarians than they are now. It was a time of "spare the rod and spoil the child" and "children should be seen and not heard." It is possible that his parents were stricter on him because he was a problem child. They may simply have been trying to make him conform to what they considered to be normal behavior in the only way that they knew.

It is important to remember that unruly children were handled by their parents, not psychologists, and that medications to control certain behaviors were not available. If a child was viewed as unruly or rebellious, parents, as well as the community, would most certainly have felt that a strong disciplinary course of action was needed.

Therefore, what Cochran viewed as meanness and lack of affection may have been his parents' method of dealing with what they saw as a troublesome child.

Cochran's inability to relate or interact favorably with others most certainly carried over into his adulthood. Although he would have been considered to be an attractive man at five feet, eleven inches tall, lanky build, dark hair and swarthy complexion, he never married. Though he stated that his mother wanted him to marry (another effort at making him conform to the norm), he had a marked hostility toward women, especially scantily clad women. He stated to a psychiatrist that women did not wear enough clothes and that seeing them dressed in shorts or a bathing suit upset him "extremely and emotionally."

Though it is a matter of record that Cochran never married, and apparently had never formed a lasting relationship with a woman, it is interesting to note that when a deputy questioned him as to whether he had normal sexual relations, his answer was that he "had two wives and two children and another woman pregnant," indicating a defensiveness in this regard.

Willie Grady Cochran was a dichotomy. He has been described by those who knew him as "mean as hell," "an interesting man," "evil," and "not scared of anything in this world." Yet, reading the testimony of those that spoke with him and spent time with him after his arrest and during his trial, he appears polite, humble, and sometimes pathetic. There are times when one is almost able to feel sympathy for him, until remembering the horror of his crime, knowing what he was capable of doing, and believing in heart and mind that he would do it again.

Willie Grady had been plagued most of his life by mental illness, with periods of seeming normalcy, and he was insightful enough about his illness to be aware of the danger.

Willie Grady began his criminal career early in life. At the age of twenty-one, he received his first criminal conviction. He was living in Rome, Georgia, and was employed by Tubize Corporation, later called Celanese Corporation. This was known in the area as the "silk mill" because of its production of silk fiber products. On January 11, 1940, he was convicted of forgery and sentenced to twelve months. Thus, began a criminal history with a multitude of convictions.

Following his conviction in January 1940, Cochran escaped on June 3, 1940, and was not recaptured until June 21, 1943. During this three-year period, he was convicted of crimes in two other states: violation of the Dyar Act in both Idaho and Texarkana, Arkansas, and forgery in Idaho. (The Dyar Act involves taking stolen motor vehicles across state lines.) He received a sentence of eighteen months and served a term in the Leavenworth Federal Penitentiary.

After his recapture on June 21, Cochran escaped again on June 25, 1943. No mention is made of his recapture, but he was sentenced to ten years for robbery by force, in Glynn County, Georgia on September 24, 1943.

He escaped on May 6, 1944 and remained at large until June 22, 1944. On July 13, 1945, he escaped again, only to be recaptured the same day. Five days later, on July 18th, he was convicted of auto theft and armed robbery - a five-year sentence for the first and a twenty-year sentence for the second.

Both these crimes were in Floyd County, Georgia and involved the armed robbery of a taxi driver. Willie Grady and another man had the cab driver take them to a rural area in Floyd County. They had the driver stop and Willie Grady forced him, at gunpoint, to get out of the cab. The two men made the driver take off his clothes, tied him to a tree with his belt, and stuffed his shirt in his mouth. Cochran pointed his gun at the man and pulled the trigger, but the gun misfired. The driver managed to free himself, run to a house nearby and call the police. Cochran and his companion were arrested a short time later while driving the taxi.

Following the convictions in Floyd County, he was convicted the next month (August 23, 1945) of rape in Bartow County, Georgia and sentenced to twenty years. Details of the rape are sketchy. The newspaper account states the father of the victim swore out a warrant and served as prosecutor. It also states that the victim was from a prominent Bartow County family and that

Cochran was found guilty of "striking, beating and wounding" the victim.

Other sources state that Cochran took the young woman to a wooded area where he raped her, beat her and tied her to a tree. According to these sources, he kept her there for two or three days and she was found by rabbit hunters.

Fourteen months later, October 1946, there was another conviction for assault with intent to rape. This occurred in Gilmer County, Georgia and carried a sentence of one to two years.

All of the crimes for which he was convicted, subsequent to the first one for forgery, were, apparently, committed during the period of his escapes, either between 1940-1943 or 1944-1945.

After his conviction for rape in Bartow County, Cochran was sent to Georgia State Prison in Tattnall County, Georgia. This was the prison for the worst of the worst in Georgia. Most of the incorrigibles were housed there. During his incarceration there, there was an incident in which he got into a fight with another inmate and attempted to kill him. He was sent to the state mental hospital at Milledgeville for evaluation and determined to be psychotic in August 1948. He was transferred from the prison to the state hospital in September of that year, where he remained until February, 1950. At that time, he was declared free of psychosis and returned to prison, where he remained until he was paroled on December 24, 1954. Two previous requests for parole had been denied.

Upon his release from prison, Willie Grady Cochran rode the train to his home in Paulding County, Georgia. On the trip home, he got into a fight with another passenger and broke the man's arm. Once home he found work at a local sawmill. He remained in Paulding County until his arrest on June 22, 1955, an arrest from which he would neither escape nor ever see his home again.

Priscilla Sullins & Connie Baker

CHAPTER 3

Patricia Ann Cook was born to John and Ruby Baugh Cook on January 31, 1941. She was Ruby's second child and second daughter, and John's first child and only daughter. Patricia's half sister, Mary Ann, was four years older. Patricia was a quiet, sweet child who adored her family.

Before Patricia was seven, her parents had divorced. Her father re-married and had a son, Danny, in 1948. Her mother also re-married and Patricia lived with her mother and stepfather, J. C. "Bud" Waters. She was devoted to her family and enjoyed a close relationship with all of them. She often spent time with her father and his family.

Patricia began elementary school at Eighth Ward School. By this time, she was "Pat" or "Patsy" to her friends and to her extended family. In school, she excelled academically and was described by teachers as a model student and far above average intelligence. She was blonde, blue-eyed and popular with her classmates. In sixth grade she was Eighth Ward's "May Queen."

In the fall of 1954, Patricia began her first year at Rome Junior High School. The junior high at that time included grades seven, eight and nine, and students transferred to Rome High School in the tenth grade. Seventh grade, then as now, was a time for socialization and budding adolescence.

Though the junior and senior high schools were in separate buildings, the school yearbook, "The Roman," included all grades, seven through twelve. In 1954, Patricia was elected by the 650-member student body as one of twelve "favorites" of both schools.

The 1954-55 school year was a busy and exciting year for Patricia. She began taking piano lessons and played in the Drum and Bugle Corps at school. During football season high school bands marched in parades down Broad Street every Friday afternoon at 4 o'clock.

When Patricia went to the Teen Club on Friday nights, she was pleasantly surprised when she was often asked to dance. (A man, now in his sixties, remembers a crush he had on the beautiful, blue-eyed, blonde.)

During that school year, Patricia rode the bus to school, and each morning the bus would pass the dry cleaners where her mother worked. Patricia would always wave and yell, "Bye, Mama!" as it passed. Soon, all of the children on the bus joined in and would yell, "Bye, Mama!" along with her.

In the summer of 1955, Patricia had completed her first year of junior high school. She had made excellent grades, participated in school activities and was popular and well liked by her peers. That year she was the only child living with her mother and "Bud" Waters. Mary Ann had married and was with her husband, who was in the Army, stationed in Germany.

As the summer vacation began, Patricia was content. Although still retaining parts of her childhood, she was emerging into young womanhood. She helped with housework and often started supper for her mother. She was leaving girlhood behind that summer.

She loved to read, and she also wrote poetry. In 1953, she had composed a Mother's Day poem for her mother. Her other interests included collecting unique salt and pepper shakers which

You Can't Play Outside...

she displayed in a cabinet in her home. That summer she enjoyed visiting friends and swimming at Roy's pool, only a few blocks away. Her only fear in life was thunderstorms. Patricia was terrified of thunderstorms.

She was a responsible and considerate child and never left her home without calling her mother or leaving a note. On Monday, June 20th, 1955, all that changed forever.

When the thunderstorms of July and August came in 1955, John Cook, remembering his daughter's fears, could be seen sitting beside her grave, drenched yet vigilant.

In September of that year, Ruby Waters, knowing she would never hear "Bye, Mama!" again, couldn't watch the school bus pass.

In 1941, when John and Ruby Cook brought their newborn daughter home from the hospital Willie Grady Cochran had already served time for his first felony conviction. As Patricia grew and blossomed into a pretty and happy young girl, Willie Grady continued his troubled criminal career. It would have been hard for anyone to imagine that the two would ever meet, but it was to be their destiny. Their one encounter would link them forever.

Priscilla Sullins & Connie Baker

CHAPTER 4

As Patricia Ann Cook slumbered soundly on Monday morning, June 20th, Willie Grady Cochran arose early and was making his way to Rome. He was on the road by six-thirty. He wouldn't be working at the sawmill that day. He had some business to take care of with his brother at the prison. After that, he'd have the whole day to himself.

Patricia was still sleeping peacefully as Willie Grady was conducting his business with his brother. She had a dental appointment later, but it was still early. Her stepmother, Dorothy, would not pick her up until mid-morning.

Willie Grady left the prison at about nine a.m. with his paperwork for the truck. Patricia was out of bed by that time and preparing for her dental appointment.

Dorothy Cook arrived to take Patricia to her appointment while Willie Grady was driving aimlessly around Rome, making several stops.

When Patricia arrived home from the dentist around noon, the sun was blazing. It would be a a good day to work on her tan. She called her mother at work to let her know that she was home and that she was going to "lay out in the sun" for awhile.

She was in the yard when she heard the truck slow, then stop in front of her house. She got up to look toward the front of the house and saw the man walking to her front door. She picked up her robe and walked through the house toward the front.

At the sound of the first knock, she opened the door and innocently looked up into the last face she would ever see.

Bud Waters arrived at his home at 618 East Nineteenth Street a little after five o'clock in the afternoon on Monday, June 20th, 1955.

When he got out of his car, there was a man and his two sons waiting for him. The man was interested in buying his boat and Waters did not go directly into his house but walked, with the man and boys, into the garage. They looked at the boat Waters had for sale, discussed it, and negotiated a price. Ruby had spoken with him during the day and had told him that Patricia would start supper that evening.

When the man left, Waters went into the kitchen. He did not see Patricia or any sign that supper had been started. He walked through the house and into the back yard, calling her name. When he could find no sign of her, he called his wife at work.

"Ruby, didn't you say Patsy was home and would start supper?" he asked.

"Yes, I talked to her around one thirty or two. John's wife brought her home from the dentist. She said she was going to sunbathe and then start supper. Why? What's wrong?"

Bud calmly replied, "Nothing probably, but she's not home and it doesn't look like she began cooking, either."

Ruby Waters did not know what to think. It was so unlike Patricia to do something like that. Patricia always called her at work to let her know if she was going somewhere. She'd also leave notes on the coffee table saying where she was and how to get in touch with her.

You Can't Play Outside...

Ruby told her husband, "I'll call her girlfriends and see if she's there or if they know where she might be and call you back. Look on the coffee table, too. You know she leaves notes there."

She phoned several of Patricia's close friends, but they had not heard from her at all.

Ruby began to feel uneasy. She called her husband and told him to come get her at work. Bud went to the cleaners where his wife worked, and they headed home. They discussed what could have happened and why Patricia would go somewhere without letting them know or leaving a note. Bud was becoming increasingly worried, but attempted to soothe his wife.

"Something just came up, or someone came by. You know how teenagers can be. She probably lost track of time. Maybe she'll be there when we get home."

But Ruby said, "Bud, you know how good Patsy is. She'd never go off like that."

When the Waters returned to their home, there was still no sign of Patricia. They went to her room and looked through her closet. They could find nothing missing except her bathing suit and her flowered robe. They went again to the back yard. There in the back yard was a quilt, a pillow and a bottle of sun tan lotion.

Ruby and Bud called more of Patricia's friends. No one had heard from her since around one o'clock.

"Bud, go to Roy's, maybe she got a ride to the pool, maybe someone there saw her. Go ask there. Please."

Ruby was becoming increasingly agitated. She paced the floor and waited for her husband's return. She heard footsteps on the front porch. Maybe he'd found her. She opened the door to see her husband.

"Nothing. Nobody at the pool remembers seeing her today. The neighbors I talked to said she'd been sunbathing."

It was nearing seven in the evening and Patricia had never been out this late, unless she had her parents' permission to attend a party or movie. Ruby phoned her ex-husband, J.D. Cook.

"Patsy's not home. We've called everyone we can think of. Bud's been to Roy's and all around the neighborhood. Nobody's seen Patsy since she came home with Dorothy from the dentist.

She called me and told me she'd be in the back yard sunbathing. Did she call you?"

Cook didn't know what to think. Neither he nor his wife had heard from Patricia. He was concerned because it was so late and so unlike his daughter to cause her family to worry.

"I think you should call the police, Ruby," said John Cook. "There's probably a good explanation for this, but it's getting late and we need to see what's going on."

Bud called the Rome City Police Department and reported his fourteen year old stepdaughter's absence. Shortly afterwards, Detective Bill Terhune arrived at 618 East Nineteenth Street.

"Was Patricia having any problems? Was she in trouble with you or her stepparents for anything?" the detective asked.

"No," began Ruby, "Patsy has a good relationship with my husband. She's crazy about her daddy, and she and John's wife get along just fine. They have a son, Danny, and Patsy loves playing with him. It's not like Patsy to be out without letting us know where she is. I'm so afraid something's wrong."

Ruby began to cry.

Bud opened a drawer in the coffee table, "Look here, Detective Terhune. These are all notes that Patsy left when she was just going down the street. We've called all her friends and her daddy. I've been to Roy's pool and asked neighbors. No one seems to have seen or talked to Patsy since around one thirty this afternoon."

Detective Terhune assured the Waters he would do everything possible to find their daughter. After getting a description of Patricia and what clothes she was believed to have been wearing, he returned to the police department. He called his boss, Chief Smith Horton, at home.

CHAPTER 5

"Chief, I think we got a problem. A girl's been reported missing from the East Rome area. I've just been to her home. Nobody's heard from this girl since early afternoon. I can't see anything suspicious about her home life. Everybody I've talked to says she's not the type to run off or stay out without permission."

Detective Terhune and Chief Horton decided to put out an all points bulletin for the girl. County Sheriff Joe Adams was notified and both agencies began searching for any sign of Patricia Ann Cook.

Neighbors and friends who had heard about Patricia's disappearance came by the Waters' home to offer comfort and assistance. The women stayed with Ruby and some of the men formed an unofficial search party. They had shotguns and began searching for Patricia right before dark. They made their way to Chulio Road, stopping at an area known as Lover's Lane. They found no trace of her.

During the police investigation that evening it was learned that a trio of teenage boys had left that afternoon on a trip to Tennessee and Virginia. One of the boys was known to have admired Patricia and had stated to friends that he might not be traveling alone on his trip. Police questioned the boy's parents and verified that he had left that evening with two friends. The boy's father provided police with his license plate number. Tennessee authorities were alerted and the boys were subsequently located and taken into custody in Rockwood, Tennessee on Wednesday the 23rd. They were held briefly for interrogation but were released when Georgia officials notified them that the boys had no connection with the Cook case. By that time, a more likely suspect was already in custody.

By Tuesday morning, the situation had begun to look ominous. Rome City Police Detectives, William Terhune and Oscar Williams went to Chief of Police Smith Horton with their findings.

"Went through the usual routine," they reported. "We've searched lakes and swimming holes, questioned her friends and relatives, called every hospital within a fifty-mile radius, talked to employees at the railroad and bus terminals. Nothing."

"What about her background? How'd she get along with her folks?" the Chief asked.

"We checked into that," Terhune said. "Her mother is remarried and her stepfather, Bud Waters, is crazy about her. Her father, John Cook, is remarried and he and his wife also have a good relationship with her. As a matter of fact, it was her stepmother who took her to the dentist yesterday morning. I couldn't find anything wrong with either one."

"What about her room?"

"Searched it. Nothing. All her clothes and make-up are there. Her wallet was on the dresser with a few dollars in it. The only thing missing is the bathing suit that she had on and a flowered housecoat that she used for a beach robe."

The Chief knew, as did the detectives, that the situation was not looking good. All of the normal avenues for a missing person had been explored and had turned up nothing. They knew in their gut as police officers often do, that something was not right.

You Can't Play Outside...

Everyone that they had spoken with, parents, teachers, and friends, had portrayed Patricia as a model child and student. She was shy and retiring, yet popular. She had gone to the movies and dances with boys but had no steady boyfriend. She was above average intelligence and made good grades. She conscientiously left notes for her mother whenever she went somewhere.

"No," thought the Chief, "this is definitely not a runaway."

He could tell by the serious expression on the face of each of his detectives that they felt the same dread that he did.

Pictures of Patricia were sent to all law enforcement agencies east of the Mississippi and the three radio stations in Rome were given her description, which they aired every thirty minutes. The local newspaper was also covering the story and planned to print her picture on the front page that day.

After their conference at the station, the Chief and the two detectives decided to go to East Nineteenth Street and talk to the neighbors. They stopped at 620 East Nineteenth Street, the home of Myrtle Scoggins. She told the officers that she had indeed seen Patricia on Monday afternoon at about two forty-five.

"I was visiting my neighbor when I heard a car start up," she said. "I looked out the front window of the house because I thought it might be my husband coming in and that's when a truck passed by and I recognized Patsy inside, on the passenger side."

"You didn't see her get in the truck?" one of the detectives asked.

"No, I didn't look outside until I heard it start up."

"What kind of truck was it, Mrs. Scoggins?"

"I don't know the body style, all I know is that it looked like it was a light gray truck."

This was their first real clue. The officers thanked Mrs. Scoggins and moved on down the street, going door to door. A couple of blocks away at 406 East Nineteenth Street, they spoke with Jane Kinsey. She reported to the officers that she had been sweeping her front porch Monday afternoon, sometime after two o'clock, when a pickup truck stopped in front of the house and a man got out. He came into the yard and asked her if she knew a family by the name of Crawford.

"I told him that I didn't know any Crawfords, but that my aunt was inside laying down and I would go ask her, so I did. She didn't know them either and I went back outside and told him that."

"What did he say?"

"He said that he'd have to look somewhere else."

"What did he do, then? Did he say anything else?" asked the detective.

"No, he didn't say anything else. He got in his truck and drove off."

"What kind of truck was it?"

"It was a light gray pickup."

"What did this man look like?"

"He was tall, slim and dark complected," Jane Kinsey said.

"How old do you think he was?" Williams asked.

"I'd say he was in his thirties," she replied.

Checking on both sides of the street, the officers could find no one who remembered a family named Crawford ever living on the street.

Chief Horton, Williams and Terhune discussed what they had learned over lunch at a nearby cafe.

"Seems to me," Chief Horton said, "this man in the pickup truck was casing the neighborhood when he happened up on the girl at home by herself."

"Well, if he took her, it couldn't have been for ransom because her family's not rich," one of the detectives observed.

The other officers agreed and Chief Horton said, "I think it might be a good idea to check our records for every morals offender in the county."

Back at the station, they began the process of identifying those offenders. At the same time, they notified law enforcement in the surrounding counties to do the same.

That afternoon the local newspaper, *The Rome News Tribune*, ran a picture of Patricia Ann Cook on the front page along with an article about her disappearance. The article gave the information that she had been seen the previous afternoon with a man in a light gray pickup truck. This prompted several telephone calls to the police regarding sightings of the pair or the truck.

Soon after dark on Tuesday, a service station attendant called to report that he gassed a green 1955 Ford pickup truck on Monday afternoon at about one o'clock. He said that the driver was alone and when asked to describe him, he gave a description that fit the one given earlier by Jane Kinsey. Seeking to gain any information about the driver, the police asked the attendant if they had had any conversation.

The attendant said, "He didn't have much to say, just that he liked Rome because it was such a pretty town."

The first real break came later that night when a farm couple called to report that they had seen a man and a girl walking into the woods near their home in the Mullinax Mountain area of Bartow County.

When asked for a description of the pair, the farmer said, "Well, the man was tall with dark hair and the girl was blonde. She had on a bathing suit."

"Did you see them come back out of the woods?" the police asked.

"No, we were busy, but I heard a car crank up about an hour after I saw them go into the woods."

"Did you see the vehicle? Was it a car or a truck?"

"I don't really know, I never saw it, just heard it."

"Can you show us where it was?"

"Yessir, I can," the farmer replied.

With that, arrangements were made to meet with the farmer early the next morning at first light.

Chief Horton telephoned Sheriff Atwood in Bartow County to let him know they would be in his county the next morning. He gave Atwood the details and location of the sighting. Sheriff Atwood said he would send men out that night to search.

Priscilla Sullins & Connie Baker

CHAPTER 6

Early Wednesday morning, Williams and Terhune left for Bartow County to meet with the farmer and look over the area where he had seen the couple go into the woods. The wooded area had been searched during the night by Sheriff Frank Atwood of Bartow County and other searchers. They had located a cabin in the woods with empty drink bottles, but no other signs of occupancy.

"Can you show us where you think you heard the vehicle?" they asked the farmer.

He took them to an area that he thought it might have been and there were tire prints and footprints there. Immediately, they sent for a laboratory technician to make plaster casts of the tire prints.

Meanwhile, back in Floyd County, Chief Horton was told by an officer that a young man was waiting to see him.

"What does he want?" the Chief asked.

"He says that he has some information about the Cook case," the officer replied.

"Okay, send him in."

The young man walked into the Chief's office and sat down.

The Chief said, "They say you have some information on the Cook case."

"Yessir. I know a guy that fits the description of the man you think she might have been seen with and I know that he was aggravating some of the girls in front of the school a few months ago, and Patsy was one of them. In fact, he sort of picked on her in particular."

"How do you know all this?" the Chief asked.

"Well sir, my sister told me about it. She's in Patsy's class at school and we know him because he used to be a neighbor of ours. My sister said that he was pestering Patsy so much that she had to go back inside the school to get away from him. His name is Henry Smith."

"Do you know where we can find him?"

"I don't know where he lives, but I think he hangs out at a pool hall on Broad Street. Somebody there will probably know where he lives."

Broad Street was the main street in Rome's downtown area. There were three pool halls on Broad Street. The most popular one, Hill City Pool Room, was located in the basement of the Forrest Hotel. Two others were on the Cotton Block, at the south end of Broad. These were on opposite sides of the street and occupied upper floors.

"Which pool hall?"

"Vic's - over the Busy Bee Cafe."

Chief Horton thanked the man for the information and led him out. Immediately the Chief had the files checked to see if there was a police record on Smith. He found a record for a minor offense, drunk and disorderly, and learned that Smith was thirty-five years old.

Williams and Terhune returned from Bartow County shortly thereafter, so Chief Horton gave them the information and told them to check it out.

After parking on the Cotton Block, they climbed the stairs to Vic's and spoke with the manager. He told them where they could find the man that they were looking for. Leaving the pool room they drove across the Coosa River Bridge to South Broad Street.

The address was an old, Victorian house that had been converted to a rooming house. Terhune knocked on the door and when Smith opened it, the detectives identified themselves.

"Can we come in? We need to talk to you."

"What about?" asked Smith as he stepped back to let them in.

"We heard you know Patricia Ann Cook," said Williams, as the two detectives stepped into a one-room, shabbily furnished apartment.

They noticed a bed, a chair, and a hot plate on a small table.

Smith looked nervous and said, "I don't know her. I've never met her."

Williams told him what they had heard about the incident at the school and he said, "I didn't mean any harm. I was going through a bad time then. My wife had left me and I was drinking."

"We heard that you picked on Patricia in particular. Why is that?"

"I don't know. I guess because she was the prettiest, but I didn't mean anything by it. I wouldn't have hurt any of those girls. It was just a bad time for me."

"What about now?" Williams asked.

"Things are looking better. I got a job at the cafe and me and my wife are talking about getting back together."

"Where were you Monday afternoon between one and three o'clock?" Terhune asked.

"I was at work."

Williams and Terhune left the rooming house and went directly to the cafe where they verified with the owner that he had, indeed, been at work at that time. Another dead end. Discouraged, the two detectives returned to the station to report their findings to the Chief and to see if any checks of convicted morals offenders in the area had turned up anything.

Shortly after their return, the Chief received a call from the owner of a small country store in Bartow County. He told the

Chief that he had just heard about the case and that he thought that the man and the girl had stopped at his store Monday afternoon.

The Chief said to his two detectives, "Come on. Let's go. We've got another lead, sounds like a good one. Let me call Frank (Atwood) and tell him we're headed into Bartow County."

As they drove down Chulio Road toward Bartow County, they were all aware that they were heading toward the same general area where the farmer had seen the man and the girl. Crossing the line into Bartow County, the officers had traveled less than a quarter of a mile when they saw the store on the left. They pulled in and, as they were getting out of the car, a middle-aged couple, simply dressed, came out to meet them. Bartow County Sheriff Frank Atwood was already there.

After introducing themselves to each other, they all went inside the store. It was obvious that H. H. Duncan and his wife had been anxiously awaiting their arrival. Chief Horton took a picture of Patricia Ann Cook out of a folder and showed it to the couple. "Is this the girl that you saw Monday afternoon?" he asked.

H. H. Duncan took the picture, looked at it and said, "Yessir, it is."

Then he handed the picture to his wife, who looked at it and said, "Yes, that's her."

"Tell us what time you saw her and what happened," said Chief Horton.

"Well," Duncan said, "it was about four thirty in the afternoon. I was inside the store when this truck pulled up and blew the horn."

"What kind of truck? What color?"

"It was a Ford pickup truck. As to the color, well, I believe it was green, but it was dusty and the dust made it look sort of gray."

"Okay, then what happened?"

"I went to the door when I heard him blow his horn, and he said, 'Bring me two Double Colas.' I was taking them to him when he asked what the deposit on the bottles would be. I told him fifteen cents for all of it and he paid the money and left."

"Which way did he go?"

"He left going south, toward Cartersville," Duncan said.

"Did the girl say anything?"

"No sir, she was sitting on the passenger side. She just looked like she was mashed up against the door, in the corner of the truck, just as far as she could get. I never saw her move or bat her eyes or nothing."

"Mrs. Duncan, you saw the girl, too, is that right?"

"Yessir."

"What can you tell us?"

"Well, as you can see, our house is built together with the store. I was in the living room when I heard the horn blow and I stepped out onto the porch. I noticed the girl in the truck because her eyes looked awful to me. They looked like hot glass. The man was looking away from her and she wiggled her fingers at me like she wanted to tell me something. I stood there and looked at her and she kept wiggling her fingers at me, so I walked down into the yard where the truck was at and asked if there was anything else they wanted. The man said, 'No, he's helping us,' so I walked back onto the porch. I turned around and looked back at her and she was still wiggling her fingers toward me."

"What happened then?"

"He got his Double Colas and left."

"Did you see which way he went?"

"Nossir. To tell the truth, I didn't look. The way that girl looked had really hurt me and I didn't watch them leave."

The officers thanked the Duncans for the information and walked out to the Chief's car. Atwood told Horton that he would stop at other stores and gas stations on his way back to Cartersville to ascertain if the pair had been seen.

"You know, Chief, this sounds like a local guy. These are back roads and he could have even been headed to Paulding County."

There was total silence in the vehicle as the Rome officers drove away from the store, each man replaying the interview in his mind. All had the same thought, the girl was probably dead.

Arriving back at the station, the three somber officers went directly to the Chief's office. It was about two-thirty in the afternoon, almost forty-eight hours since the girl had disappeared. They were joined, almost immediately, by Sheriff Joe Adams and

Joe Burton, who was an agent with ATF (Alcohol, Tobacco, and Firearms).

According to A.L. Woody, a former deputy in Bartow County, all law enforcement was "like a big family in those days." They all worked together. Jurisdictions were not an issue as they are today, especially in cases such as this.

The Chief related to them the information that had been obtained from the Duncans.

"I know a guy that drives a green Ford pickup," Sheriff Adams said, "but he's in the Public Works Camp right now for drunk driving."

"Are you sure he's still there?" the Chief asked.

Sheriff Adams picked up the phone and said, "Well, let's just call Warden Caldwell and find out."

He spoke with the Warden and was told that Cochran was still there and that he had definitely been there on Monday because his brother, Grady, had come by to see him that morning to get some papers signed.

When Sheriff Adams told the others what the Warden had said, Joe Burton sat bolt upright and said, "Grady Cochran? I know him from my days with the Georgia State Patrol. You know, I was based in Paulding County and that's where he's from. He's a bad one, that Willie Grady, been in a lot of trouble. As a matter of fact, he's been in prison for raping a girl in Bartow County and I heard that he got out a few months ago. You know, he took that girl to the woods and tied her to a tree. She was missing for several days before she was found."

All the officers looked at each other. All of the other morals offenders that they had checked out had alibis. This was one that they hadn't checked.

Chief Horton said, "I'll call the Parole Board and see what kind of information they have on Mr. Willie Grady Cochran. Joe (Sheriff Adams), you call Sheriff Wilbanks in Paulding County and see what he knows about Cochran."

When each man had completed his call, they had learned that Cochran had been paroled on December 24, 1954 and was currently employed at a sawmill near Dallas, in Paulding County. His parole officer told Chief Horton that on Cochran's last visit, he reported that he "was living a good Christian life." Sheriff Wilbanks told Joe Adams that Willie Grady had been seen driving a green Ford pickup.

An officer was sent to the home of Myrtle Scoggins with five mug shots, one of whom was Willie Grady Cochran. Mrs. Scoggins, who had seen Patricia leaving with a man on Monday afternoon, picked Cochran's picture out of the group. The officer used Mrs. Scoggins' phone to relay this information to Chief Horton.

As the officer stepped off Mrs. Scoggins' porch, he saw Bud Waters coming across the yard toward him.

When he reached the bottom step, Waters met him and asked, "Do you have any news? I'm on my way to Floyd Hospital. My wife was admitted last night. She's gone all to pieces."

The officer told Waters that Patricia had been seen leaving the area in a green Ford truck and that there had been a report of a man and a girl fitting her description stopping at a store on Chulio Road.

"Do you know anybody who drives a truck like that or who lives out that way?"

"No. What store was it?"

"Sir, I don't know which store, but the Chief and some others went out there this morning. I want you to know that we're doing everything we can to find your little girl."

"I know. I appreciate that. I just wish I had some good news to tell my wife. I'm worried about her."

"Well, sir, we'll sure let you know as soon as we know anything."

With that, the officer left and Bud Waters went directly to his car. He had to find out for himself if the girl seen at the store was Patricia. He drove toward Chulio Road and a small grocery store he remembered there.

Before he reached Mathis Grocery, his car began to overheat. By the time he arrived at the small store, clouds of steam billowed from under the hood. He stopped the car and rushed inside the store, leaving the car motor running.

"Are you the folks who saw the girl in the pickup truck Monday?"

The proprietor look puzzled and said, "I don't know what you're talking about." Waters realized it was not the right store.

"Do ya'll know of any more stores out this road?"

"There's Duncan's on down the road, right across the county line."

"Thank you," Waters said as he rushed back to his car. Ignoring the steam, he sped off toward Bartow County. He slowly realized, however, that the car would not make it much further. He reluctantly turned back toward Rome and his wife at Floyd Hospital.

When Chief Horton received the news that Mrs. Scoggins had identified Cochran, he looked at the other officers and said, "Let's go to Paulding County. I think we may have our man. We'll meet Sheriff Wilbanks at his office."

CHAPTER 7

It was after one-thirty when the officers left Floyd County en route to Paulding County. The group was comprised of Chief Horton, Terhune, Williams, Floyd Deputy Wayne Lindsey, Rome City Patrolman Paul Polston, Joe Burton (Federal ATF), and Grover Newman (State Revenue Agent). They arrived at Sheriff Grady Wilbanks' office and, after a brief meeting to apprise him of their suspicions, the group, along with Sheriff Wilbanks, headed for the sawmill where Cochran was employed.

Upon their arrival, they questioned the foreman and verified that Cochran had not been at work on Monday. He pointed to the area where Cochran was working. Willie Grady Cochran looked up and saw the approaching officers. He was holding an axe and tightened his grip. He was tense. He knew why they were there.

Chief Horton stopped several feet from him and said, "Are you Willie Grady Cochran?"

"Yeah," Cochran replied, lowering the axe but not releasing it.

"I'm the police chief in Rome. We're here to take you with us for questioning."

"What for?" Cochran asked.

Terhune, his anger apparent, stepped toward Cochran. "You know what we're here for you son of a bitch! We want to know what you did with Patricia Ann Cook!"

"I don't know what ya'll are talking about and I ain't going to Rome."

Terhune stepped closer. "Oh yeah, you're going."

Cochran began to raise the axe and was quickly surrounded and overpowered.

It was approximately three thirty in the afternoon, June 22, 1955, when he was placed in the police car with Williams, Terhune and two other officers.

Before leaving Paulding County, the remaining officers went to the home of Cochran's mother and impounded a late model green Ford pickup truck.

Cochran was quiet on the ride back to Rome. His silence fueled Terhune's growing rage. At one point Terhune suggested stopping and shooting the prisoner.

Williams told Terhune, "We can't do that, Bill. We'll never find that little girl without him."

Terhune realized that Williams was right and calmed down somewhat.

When they arrived at the Rome City Jail, located in the basement of the city auditorium building, Cochran was taken to a small room for questioning. The interrogation continued throughout the night and the next day. Cochran was stoic, refusing to make any statement.

During that evening and night, a group of more than two hundred officers and volunteers searched the area in Bartow County where it was believed that the girl was last seen. It was hoped that she might be found alive, perhaps tied up in the woods or an abandoned farmhouse.

At this time, Sheriff Adams requested the assistance of the National Guard and Company E, the Rome Guard unit, was ordered into the search by Governor Marvin Griffin. Headquarters for the search was set up at the historic Stilesboro

You Can't Play Outside...

Academy in south Bartow County. Rome police officers had been put on twenty-four hour duty. Local churches held special prayer services that night for Patricia Ann.

By noon Thursday the officers had not made any headway. Cochran would give them no information, would admit to nothing. A high-ranking city official appeared at the police department in the early afternoon and called the officers together for a meeting.

"Boys, we've got to find this little girl. If she's tied up in the woods somewhere she'll starve to death."

Williams spoke up, "We know that. We've questioned him since yesterday afternoon and he won't talk."

"Well, you're gonna have to get rough with him. You know what he did to that other girl."

"You gonna back us up on this?"

He nodded.

At the conclusion of the meeting, Cochran was brought from his cell to the small interrogation room and handcuffed to a chair. When the questioning resumed that afternoon, Willie Grady Cochran began to talk.

Finally, late in the afternoon, they put him in a police car and headed for Bartow County and the area where the girl was last seen. They stopped at Duncan's store and asked the couple if he was the man that they had seen on Monday. Both of the Duncans positively identified him. As they left the store, the officers began to hammer him with questions.

"OK, Grady, we know it was you that stopped by that store Monday and we know that you had the girl with you. You better start talking!"

Cochran started mumbling incoherently about the girl, said that he couldn't remember anything.

"You're not making any sense, Grady."

About that time, they were approaching the Etowah River Bridge near Euharlee and someone in the car said something about the river.

Suddenly, Cochran said, "That's where she is. She's in the river."

The officer that was driving slammed on the brakes and pulled over to the side of the road. They were on the Cartersville-Dallas Road, State Route 61, in Bartow County.

"What did you say? Did you say that she's in the river?"

Cochran nodded.

Every officer in the car was tense and staring at Willie Grady Cochran. For a moment, it was as if each one of them had stopped breathing and there was total silence in the vehicle. Then, they all started talking at once, firing questions at Cochran, all asking the same questions.

"Did you say that she's in the river?"

"What river?"

Cochran pointed to the bridge up ahead.

The driver started the car and pulled onto the bridge. It was late, after midnight, and there was no traffic in the area at that time of night. They stopped the car and everyone got out. Besides Chief Horton and Williams and Terhune, there were several other officers there. Sheriff Joe Adams and City Officer N.F. Duck were there, as well as two Georgia Bureau of Investigation agents and several Georgia State Troopers. All of these officers and Cochran were standing on the bridge and the interrogation became intense once again.

Just how intense is anybody's guess. Interviews with certain individuals, who were in law enforcement at the time, indicate that one of the detectives looped his belt around Cochran's neck, put his knee in his back and jerked the belt, telling him to talk. This was never a matter of public knowledge and after almost fifty years, no one was willing to absolutely confirm or be quoted on this incident.

Finally, at around two thirty in the morning, on a dark bridge crossing the Etowah River, Cochran confessed.

"I stopped at her house and knocked on the door. She came to the door wearing a bathing suit. I spoke to her and asked her if she knew where Sims Crawford lived and she said she didn't. I said, 'Young lady, it looks like you should be in swimming with a bathing suit on.' I told her that I would kinda like to be in swimming myself as hot as it is."

You Can't Play Outside...

He went on to say that he thanked her and she asked if he was going by the swimming pool. He told her that he could, and she told him to wait while she went to get her robe and shoes. Cochran told the officers that they got into his truck and drove to Roy's pool. He said they parked facing the pool and talked for a few minutes.

"I asked her if she was going in swimming, and she told me she couldn't swim. I told her that I probably couldn't swim myself because it had been so long since I had been in swimming. I told her she probably ain't got no money, and I'd pay her way in. She said she'd ride some, but that she had to get back home to cook supper."

Cochran said they left the pool and headed out Chulio Road, where they stopped twice to get Cokes. They drove into Bartow County and he pulled onto the Old Lucus Road. He said they stopped at a mud hole and after talking for a few minutes, he choked her to death.

He hid her body under some bushes and went home to Burnt Hickory where he obtained a quilt, baling wire, a log chain and a wrench. Cochran told the officers that it was dark by the time he returned to the Old Lucus Road.

"I walked into the woods where I had left her. It was too dark to see so I toted her back up to the road and laid her down."

He described wrapping her body in the quilt and weighting it with the chain and wrench.

"When I was done, I picked her up and laid her in the back of the truck. I drove to the bridge and threw her in."

Upon hearing his confession, the officers told Cochran to get back into the car and show them the way to the Old Lucus Road, which he did. At that point the officers felt they had gotten all they could from Cochran and a decision had to be made as to where to take him. The night before there had been a disturbance at the city jail. A group of about two hundred citizens, having heard of his arrest, gathered outside the jail, chanting, "Send him out!" Some were armed.

They decided to take him to the Fulton Tower (jail) in Atlanta, to be placed in a maximum security cell. Barefoot and wearing overalls, he was greeted by Atlanta newsmen, one of whom noticed that he had a black eye and questioned him about it.

"They beat me up there," he told them and then added, "Yeah, I admitted certain things."

CHAPTER 8

At dawn on Friday morning, National Guardsmen and Rome firemen began dragging the Etowah River. Sheriff Atwood of Bartow County directed the search. Allatoona Dam, near Cartersville, was kept closed to maintain a lower water level as the men formed a human chain across the river. Heavy fog hampered the search Friday morning, but by afternoon the fog had cleared and the day was blistering hot. Despite an intensive search, the body had not been found.

That morning Chief Horton had taken a warrant for Cochran for kidnapping. It would be left up to Sheriff Atwood in Bartow County to take a warrant for murder, since that crime had occurred in his county. Of course, the body would need to be found first.

That afternoon, while the search continued at the Etowah River in Bartow County, several articles and a picture of Cochran appeared in the *Rome News-Tribune*. One article concerned Cochran's parole. A parole board member was quoted as saying "it was a regular routine case." She explained that normal routine was followed, including a report from the warden at Reidsville and from the prison doctors. Cochran's physical condition was reported to be "good" and his mental condition "normal." Cochran had been visited by two parole board investigators, both recommending release.

The board member was quoted as saying, "From all reports it seemed he had a good chance for rehabilitation. He had a good prison record, and his parole record, until now, has been good."

The Parole Board asserted that Cochran had served beyond the required minimum of seven years for good behavior and met all other requirements for parole.

His picture prompted several calls to the police station from people who had seen him in Rome on Monday.

Jake Kiser, a traveling salesman who lived on East Seventh Street, called the station to tell police that he had seen Cochran between noon and one o'clock on Monday. Kiser had been loading his car to leave town when a man, who he now knew to be Cochran, parked his Ford pickup truck across the street. He never got out of the truck and was still parked there when Kiser left. His thirteen-year-old daughter Mary, said that he came to the front door of their house after her father left. It was around one o'clock, or maybe a few minutes after, when Cochran knocked on the door and asked if she knew a Mrs. Crawford. Mary told him that she didn't know anyone by that name, but that her mother was next door and she would ask her. She went back into the house and called out to her mother, asking if she knew a Mrs. Crawford. Returning to the front door, she told the stranger that neither her mother nor the neighbor knew anyone by that name. He stood there staring at her for a few minutes and she turned and went into the back of the house. When she looked back outside, the stranger and the truck were gone.

Evelyn Johnson, a black woman who worked as a domestic, reported to the police that she had been standing at the bus stop on the corner of East Second Avenue and East Eleventh Street that afternoon.

"It was about two o'clock when that white man, whose picture's in the paper, stopped and asked me about finding a young girl to work for him. I told him I didn't know of nobody and he just kept sittin' there, so I told him to give me his name and address in case I could find somebody. He seemed drunk to me, and he asked if I was sure I didn't know anybody. I told him no again and he said thanks and drove off. He never told me his name. I tell you, he made me uneasy."

Jane Kinsey also called and confirmed that Cochran was the man who stopped at her house on East Nineteenth Street sometime after two that afternoon.

As Chief Horton and the detectives discussed the fact that all of these calls placed Cochran in the vicinity of Patricia Ann Cook's home on Monday, the Chief said, "Let's check with Mable. She may know something."

Mable was a local bootlegger and madam whose house was located on the corner of East Fourteenth and Castleberry Street, only a few blocks from East Nineteenth Street. She verified that Cochran had, indeed, visited her establishment on Monday morning around eleven o'clock.

Although they had Cochran's confession and the calls placing him in the vicinity of East Nineteenth Street, the search, which had continued throughout the day, had not produced the girl's body.

Frustrated with their inability to find Patricia Ann, the officers realized that Cochran needed to be questioned again.

Sheriff Adams left for Atlanta in the wee hours of the morning and returned from Fulton Tower with Cochran in custody at about four a.m. He was taken to a cell on the top floor of the Floyd County Jail for further questioning.

"Look, Willie Grady, we've searched all day for that little girl where you told us she was and she ain't there! Now, where is she?"

"I buried her in the woods, out there on the Old Lucas Road, not far from where I killed her," Cochran replied.

Sheriff Atwood and the guardsmen were notified of this new information. They moved to the wooded area and began a thorough search there. After a while, it became apparent that this, too, would produce no results. When confronted with this information, Cochran stated that he had thrown her body into the Coosa River, off Blacks Bluff Road, below Rome.

The sheriff and other officers took him to that scene but determined fairly quickly that he was lying, so they drove him back to the Floyd County Jail for another interrogation. At this point, an assortment of officers were involved in the questioning. They included Horace Clary, Assistant Solicitor of Floyd Superior Court; Coleman Prophett, Captain and Commanding Officer of the National Guard Unit searching for the girl; Sheriff Adams; Floyd County Deputy Alton White; and Rome City Detectives Williams and Terhune.

Coleman Prophett and Deputy Alton White had prevailed upon Clary, who was also a Major in the National Guard, to go with them to the jail. Upon their arrival, they were taken directly to Cochran, who was in the cell on the top floor with Terhune and Chief of Floyd County Police, Von Brock. Clary asked them to leave so that he could speak to Cochran alone, which they did. All of the officers stayed in the background but allowed Clary to speak one on one with Cochran.

You Can't Play Outside...

CHAPTER 9

Clary began by telling Cochran, "Grady, I am a Major in the National Guard Unit that has been searching for Patricia Ann Cook. I have two purposes, one is to find her and the other is to protect you if the need arises."

Cochran's demeanor was tense, very nervous. He stared at the floor and did not speak.

Clary said, "Have a heart, Grady. The girl's mother is in the hospital because of this, and your mother is torn all to pieces. The least you could do is tell us where the body is so that the little girl can have a decent burial."

Cochran began to cry and said, "I just can't tell you."

"Grady, is she still alive?" Clary asked.

"No Major, she's not alive. She's dead," Cochran replied.

"Well, Grady, think about that girl's mother and what she's been going through. Think about your own mother. You don't have a heart in you if you don't tell us where Patricia's body is."

Still crying, Cochran turned away from Clary and looked down. He seemed to be in deep thought. Suddenly, he turned back, looked up at Clary with tears in his eyes, and asked, "Why did I do it? Why did I do it?"

"Grady, I know why you did it. You're sick."

Cochran dropped his head and didn't say anything for a while. Then, for the third time, he said, "Why did I do it?"

Clary said again, "You were sick, Grady, but you had better tell us where the little girl is."

"Well, if I could see my mother, I would tell you where she is."

"Grady, I've got good men, but they are exhausted. We have looked in the Etowah River and searched all over the mountain out there around the Old Lucas Road. Now, I want to know where she is, and then you can see your mother."

"I want to see my mother," Cochran responded.

Clary, becoming frustrated, said, "Grady, I told you that you could see your mother after you show us where the girl is. Then, I'll take you back to Fulton Tower."

Cochran sat for a minute, looking down.

Then he looked at Clary and said, "Major, you just look like a man of your word. I'll show you where she is."

"Well, Grady, I try to be a man of my word. Now, where is she?"

"She's in the river."

With this response, Clary became more exasperated and said, "That's no good, Grady. We have searched the river."

"Major, I'll show you exactly where she is."

"How can you do that, Grady? It's been several days, and with the current, how do you know where she'll be?"

"She'll be there, Major. There's a chain around her."

Cochran's demeanor changed then. He seemed to relax all over, as if a great burden had been lifted from him.

"A chain? What kind of chain?" Clary asked.

"A buckling chain. It's heavy enough to hold her there. Major, I want my money."

"What money, Grady?"

You Can't Play Outside...

"I had fifty-five dollars on me when they arrested me. I need it so I can get something cold to drink down at Fulton Tower. It's hot there."

"Well, Grady, you're entitled to that. It's your money. Are you in a hot cell at Fulton Tower?"

"All jails are hot, Major. I want my clothes, too. I want my mother to bring me my clothes, and I don't want my picture taken when we leave here."

"I'll see what I can do, Grady. I'll do the best I can."

Cochran shook hands with Clary and said, "That's a deal, Major."

He looked at Sheriff Adams, who had been standing in the background, and asked if he would guarantee his requests also. The Sheriff agreed, and they all went downstairs to the county police office.

Cochran had told them that he had thrown the body off the Milam Bridge in Bartow County, not far from the first bridge that he had told them about. Captain Prophett, of the National Guard, and another officer left to seal off the bridge from onlookers before the other officers arrived with Cochran. Crowds of people had been drawn to the river to watch the boats and the dragging efforts. Cars were parked bumper to bumper for miles along the road between the river and Cartersville.

The officers had also sent for a National Guard jacket and helmet for Cochran to wear to Bartow County. They did not want him to be recognized during the trip.

While waiting for these items to arrive, Cochran looked at Clary, Adams, Brock, and the other officers and said, "I don't know why I told the Major where she was, but it was just something that he said that caused me to tell him."

The jacket and helmet arrived and Cochran put them on before being taken outside. There were several photographers there, but as requested, none of them snapped a picture. Cochran was put in the back seat of a police car with Clary. Sheriff Adams was driving and Chief Brock was in the front passenger seat.

The conversation in the car was general as they left the jail, but it soon turned to a discussion of the best route to take to the Milam Bridge. All of the officers in the vehicle agreed that it would be better to take a different route than the officers who had gone ahead of them. At this point, Cochran told them that he could show them another way to go, that it was the route that he took on his way home to Paulding County from Rome. He took them down Rockmart Road and through a community called Wax.

As they made their way to Bartow County, Clary asked Cochran why he hadn't told them before now where the girl was and he replied, "Major, I wanted to, but I just couldn't."

He looked at the Sheriff then and said, "I wanted to tell you this morning more than anything, but I couldn't."

Riding along the back roads from Floyd County to Bartow County, Cochran seemed reluctant to discuss the crime.

Finally, Clary's curiosity got the better of him and he said, "Grady, I heard somewhere that you had a gun or bought a gun recently."

"Yes, Major, I had my gun with me that day."

"Well Grady, I'm glad you told me that. I've been wondering how you got the little girl to go with you."

"I had my gun, Major." Cochran was quiet for a minute and then said, suddenly, "I shot the little girl, Major."

Clary was startled because Cochran had told everyone that he had choked her.

He turned in the seat, looked directly at Cochran, and asked, "You shot her?"

"Yessir."

"Well, Grady, I'm glad to hear that. At least it was quick and the girl didn't have to suffer by being choked to death."

Cochran said, "I couldn't have hurt that little girl. I shot her in the back through the heart, because I didn't want her to suffer. I put the pistol in my pocket and held her head while she died. Then I laid her on her back where she would look comfortable."

Still stunned by this revelation, Clary asked, "What did you do with the gun? Did you throw it away or did you hide it?"

"I hid it at home."

"Does your mother know where it is?"

"No, I hid it from her."

"Where?"

"I hid it in a stall in the barn. It's a stall on the pond side of the barn, up under a ledge. You have to reach up under the ledge to get it."

They were nearing the area of the Milam Bridge by this time and Cochran would say nothing further about the crime or his treatment of the girl. Though roads in the vicinity had been blocked, there were still a number of people around and Clary had Cochran duck down in the seat as they passed, fearing that someone might recognize him. Public sentiment was running high and he wanted to avoid any incidents.

Finally, they arrived at the bridge. It had been blocked off by the National Guard, as well as the roads in the area. Clary commented on the fine job that his men had done in accomplishing this in a short time and how proud he was of them.

Cochran agreed and said, "You ought to be proud of your men, Major. I wish I was one of your boys. I tried to get in the Army back in the '40's, but they wouldn't take me because of my record."

By this time, Sheriff Adams had stopped the car and they all got out. As they walked toward the bridge, Cochran told Clary several times that he would "live up to his word" and that Clary could depend on it. Walking onto the bridge with Clary and the others, Cochran kept his head down and seemed to be counting the posts. At the center, he stopped and took two steps forward. He looked to the left, in the direction from which they had come, and seemed to be counting the posts on the bridge again. Then he stepped forward, looked down at the river and pointed to a spot directly below.

"Major, she is right there," he said. "That chain is on her. She will be there."

There were approximately forty people, including Floyd County and Bartow County law enforcement officers and National Guardsmen, who saw where Cochran had pointed. Clary told Sheriff Adams, Sheriff Atwood and the others that he was going to take Cochran back to Fulton Tower, and they proceeded back to the car. Clary's intentions were to get Cochran away from the bridge but stay in the area until he received word as to whether the body had been found. Sheriff Adams, Bartow

Deputy A. L. Woody, and another officer went with Clary and Cochran. They moved slowly away toward Cartersville but turned onto a dirt road which would come out in Emerson, a small community just below Cartersville, toward Atlanta.

Cochran said, "Major, I am good for my word, she is there. They will find her before we get to Cartersville."

But they didn't. They radioed Clary and told him to stop and call Rome to get some divers because the water was about eight or nine feet deep.

Cochran, hearing this, said, "I didn't know that the water was that deep. I'm sorry."

They stopped the car and Adams and Woody got out at a farmhouse to make the call to Rome. After a few minutes, they returned to the vehicle and started toward Emerson again. They had not gone far when the radio came on and informed them that they had found the body.

Cochran turned toward Clary and said, "Major, I told you I was good for my word."

At that point, they proceeded to Atlanta and Fulton Tower. The conversation in the car was, at first, general. Cochran talked about his plan to buy a tractor-trailer rig and haul freight. He said that he had planned to go to Atlanta or Chicago to check on it "before this came up."

Then he said, "Major, my mother knew that I did this before I did. I can't believe that I did such a thing again. I'm sorry for the trouble that I've caused. I just wish that there was some way that people like me could be stopped."

Just before they arrived at Fulton Tower he said, "Well, Major, all of ya'll can go home and get a good night's sleep tonight. If you're ever down here in Atlanta, come to see me."

You Can't Play Outside...

CHAPTER 10

Back at the river, dragging procedures had begun as soon as Cochran was taken away from the area. Obtaining ropes and grappling hooks from police cars, Floyd County Officer Herman Evans and Special Deputy Carl Green rowed to the center of the river. At first, they were unable to locate anything due to the depth of the water. That is when the message was sent to call for the divers, but the effort was continued.

Soon, one of the men called out that he had snagged something. Slowly and carefully they pulled it close to the surface, close enough to see that it was the body. Evans, fearing that it would break loose, stripped to his underwear and jumped into the water. He took hold of the body and guided it to the riverbank where an ambulance was waiting. The body was put on a stretcher and taken to Owen Funeral Home. Sheriff Atwood had requested that the autopsy be performed by Dr. Herman D. Jones, Director of the Crime Laboratory of the State of Georgia.

Newspaper photographers were at the river and took pictures of Patricia Ann Cook's body that would later appear in Bartow County's local newspapers.

As soon as the body was removed from the scene, the roadblocks were lifted and hundreds of people swarmed the area.

Meanwhile, officers left for Cochran's home in Paulding County to search for the .38 caliber pistol that he had told them he had used to shoot the girl and had hidden there. Having his directions as to where it was hidden, they located it fairly quickly. While there they spoke with his mother, telling her of his request for his clothes and that he wanted to see her. She refused to go, saying that she was too upset and that she would go to see him later.

Back in Bartow County at Owen Funeral Home, Dr. Herman Jones was met by Dr. Harvey Howell, a Cartersville physician who was to assist with the autopsy.

When they entered the autopsy room, the body was still on the stretcher in the zippered bag in which it had been placed at the river. The zipper had been partially pulled down, and the head and part of the chest were exposed. It had been opened so that Nancy Jones, who knew Patricia Ann Cook, could identify her. She was in Cartersville and had stopped by the funeral home after hearing of the recovery of the body. She told them that she had known Patricia for about a year and was able to make a positive identification.

Dr. Jones walked over to the stretcher and pulled the zipper down, exposing the body completely. It was wrapped in a thick quilt from the chin down to the ankles. A logging chain was wrapped around the waist five times with a heavy, Stillson wrench attached to the right side with baling wire. Further examination revealed that the chain ran up the back from the waist to the neck and was tightly looped once around the neck. The end of the chain was wired to a hook at the end of the wire. Looking down to the ankles, the doctors noted that the quilt was fastened around them with baling wire, first looped around the ankle and then threaded through the quilt, holding it tightly around the legs.

As the examination progressed, Sheriff Atwood, Chief Brock, Carl Green, and Herman Evans arrived from Paulding County

You Can't Play Outside...

with the gun and a box of six .38 caliber shells. The gun was loaded with six unspent cartridges.

The doctors were just removing the quilt from the body. They saw the flowered housecoat with all seven buttons buttoned and removed it, revealing a faded red bathing suit. Slipping the front of the suit down slightly, a large wound in the left chest was observed. Looking at the suit again, they saw a hole in the front of the left side. They removed the bathing suit and the body was turned so that they could look at the back, where a small wound was noted. This was determined to be the entry wound which pierced the heart before exiting the body. The cause of death was traumatic injury to the heart with excessive bleeding.

In addition to the fatal injury to the heart, there was evidence of bruising to the neck just above the collarbone. There was also a more severe bruise to the front of the left shoulder just under the collarbone. These bruises were determined to have occurred prior to death.

The examination had now reached the point of checking for evidence of rape. Dr. Jones asked everyone to leave the room except Dr. Howell, and a vaginal smear was done. The swab was placed in a glass tube to be taken back to the crime lab by Dr. Jones for analysis.

The quilt, bathing suit, and housecoat were placed on a sheet on the floor, wrapped, and put in a large box which Dr. Jones took back to Atlanta with him.

The autopsy was complete and Patricia Ann Cook's body was released for burial.

Priscilla Sullins & Connie Baker

You Can't Play Outside...

CHAPTER 11

As Willie Grady Cochran sat in a maximum security cell in Fulton Tower in Atlanta, the local newspapers in Floyd and Bartow Counties were filled with accounts of his crime and the discovery of the body.

The Rome News Tribune quoted him as saying, when asked why he killed the girl, "I don't know. I just had an urge to kill."

This quote was part of a long and detailed account of the events of the past week as they unfolded and also included a reiteration of Cochran's criminal history.

It was reported that he had been charged with kidnapping in Floyd County and murder in Bartow County and that both grand juries were to meet on July 11th for his indictment on these charges. Based on the autopsy report from the state crime lab a charge of rape was also issued.

One small blurb, that of Chief Horton denying that Cochran received a black eye while incarcerated in Floyd County, was included in the paper as a separate article. Though Cochran had told reporters in Atlanta on Friday that he had received the black eye in Rome, the Chief stated that he did not know where it happened and that Cochran was never mistreated at any time while in Rome or Floyd County jails.

According to the newspaper the reward money that had been contributed was to go to Patricia's family. Three hundred dollars had been given by employees of the General Electric Plant where her stepfather was employed. Other contributions were made by the Rome Shrine Club, local businesses and private citizens. All totaled thirteen hundred, sixty one dollars. The reward had been declined by all law enforcement personnel and volunteers, who requested that it be given to her family.

Patricia Ann Cook's obituary appeared in the newspaper on Sunday. Her funeral was set for Monday afternoon at two o'clock at Calvary Baptist Church. It listed her survivors and reported that her mother had been hospitalized since her disappearance and that her sister was expected from Germany on that day or the next.

On Monday, Cochran was taken from Fulton Tower to the state crime lab where he was questioned by Solicitor Erwin Mitchell regarding the items found on the body of Patricia Ann Cook.

Upon being shown the wrench, the chain, the baling wire, and the quilt, Cochran was asked by Mitchell, "Do you recognize these items, Grady?"

Cochran responded, "Yeah."

"Where did you get them?" Mitchell asked.

"I went back home and got 'em."

Cochran was then shown the bathing suit and flowered housecoat and asked by Mitchell, "Do you recognize these, Grady? Is this what the girl had on?"

He answered, simply, "Yes."

After identifying all of the items at the Crime Lab, Cochran was interviewed again by Sheriff Joe Adams and other Rome officers. He admitted to them that he took Patricia Ann Cook from her home on Monday, June 20th, drove to Bartow County, shot her, and threw her body into the river. He would not,

You Can't Play Outside...

however, sign a written confession so he was taken back to Fulton Tower to await his trial in Bartow County.

Meanwhile, the funeral that had been planned for Patricia that afternoon had to be postponed until four o'clock the following afternoon as her sister had not yet arrived from Germany. The Shanklin-Attaway Post of the American Legion in Rome, along with Congressman Henderson Lanham, had made arrangements with the Department of the Army to have her returned, but there was a delay and it was learned that she would not arrive until Tuesday, the 28th. Not only was she being returned for the funeral, but her husband was being reassigned to Ft. Benning, Georgia, so that she could be closer to her mother.

On that same day, a notice appeared in the *Daily Tribune News* in Cartersville, Georgia, that pictures of Patricia Ann Cook's body were available at the newspaper office. These were pictures taken at the river as her body was brought out. The notice advised that orders could be placed at the newspaper office and that mail orders would also be accepted.

The next day funeral services were held for Patricia Ann Cook. Patricia's sister, Mary Ann, and her husband, arrived from Frankfurt, Germany approximately one hour before the funeral on Tuesday. Ruby Waters was released from the hospital that day so that she could attend her daughter's service.

The church was filled to capacity, as there were hundreds of people there to pay their respects. A profusion of wreaths and floral arrangements banked the walls of the sanctuary. Satin ribbons, stretched across the wreaths, carried messages from school groups, friends and family in heartbreakingly glittered letters.

When the service was over, the procession making its way to the cemetery was comprised of more than sixty vehicles. They slowly made their way to Oaknoll, a new cemetery on the Alabama Highway on the outskirts of Rome. Patricia would be the first person to be buried there.

And so it was, that late Tuesday afternoon, June 28th, one week and one day after her disappearance, fourteen-year-old Patricia Ann Cook was finally laid to rest. She would never attend a prom nor graduate from high school. She would never marry and have a family, but for everyone who had lived through the horror of the last week in this small, quiet southern town, she would never be forgotten.

CHAPTER 12

On June 29th, 1955, a preliminary hearing was held at the Bartow County Courthouse in Cartersville, Georgia. Willie Grady Cochran was brought before Judge J. H. Paschall on the matter of his representation by counsel. Cochran stated to the judge that he had no money to pay for an attorney to represent him. Judge Paschall asked him if he wished the court to appoint him a lawyer and Cochran replied that he did. The Judge then appointed Jere White and Marion Corbitt as his lawyers for the trial.

Jere White, now a retired Superior Court Judge, was a young attorney in 1955, having opened his practice in 1952.

Judge White said, "1952 was the beginning of my starvation period. That's not the case now, but it was then."

In 1955, Jere White had a wife and two young daughters, ages five and three. According to White, court appointed attorneys were not paid for their services in those days, except in capital murder cases. He stated that was how new lawyers gained courtroom experience. However, since this was a capital murder case, he and his fellow appointed lawyer, Marion Corbitt (now deceased), were each paid one hundred fifty dollars for their services.

Though court-appointed, Judge White remembered being accosted on the street regarding his role in the case.

The young attorneys were asked, "How can you defend this man?"

Defending Cochran was neither enviable nor popular.

After being appointed, their first order of business was to visit Cochran's mother in Paulding County and ascertain as to whether the family intended to hire an attorney. They were told by Mrs. Cochran that the family did not have the money to do so. Thus, they began their defense.

On July 11th, 1955, the Bartow County grand jury indicted Willie Grady Cochran for the murder and rape of Patricia Ann Cook. This was the first the defense had heard of the rape charge. National Guard Major Horace Clary, assistant solicitor general of the Rome Circuit, was named as prosecutor in both the murder and rape charges. However, because of his capacity as a National Guardsman and his role in the investigation of the case, he was disqualified from serving. Solicitor General Erwin Mitchell of the Cherokee circuit would try the case with the assistance of Mr. Beverly Langford.

Willie Grady Cochran was indicted, on that same day, of kidnapping by the Floyd County grand jury since the actual kidnapping occurred in Floyd County. Rome Circuit Solicitor General Chastine Parker stated that the kidnapping charge would await the outcome of the Bartow County murder trial.

During that same week the Seventh District members of the Georgia House of Representatives met in Rome to discuss the revision of Georgia parole regulations. Then Governor Marvin Griffin named Floyd County Representative Robert L. Scoggins, of Rome, as chairman of a committee consisting of these Seventh District members. Governor Griffin charged the committee to recommend that the legislature tighten state parole regulations governing sex offenders and habitual criminals.

You Can't Play Outside...

Also in that week, Cochran and another prisoner wrecked plumbing in their cell at Fulton Tower. A sink was ripped off the wall and Cochran covered a length of pipe with a torn sheet and attacked his cellmate. The fight was allegedly due to a misunderstanding about telephone privileges.

On July 14th, 1955, the trial of Willie Grady Cochran began at the Bartow County Courthouse. Cochran had been brought from Fulton Tower in Atlanta, where he was being held. He rode in a state patrol car accompanied by a convoy of ten police vehicles. Arthur Lee Woody, a Bartow County deputy, went each morning to Atlanta to pick up Cochran. Willie Grady arrived in Cartersville around seven o'clock that morning with no incident. Thirty state troopers were positioned in and around the courthouse to keep order. According to Deputy Woody, they formed a circle around the courthouse until Cochran was inside.

Cochran was kept in a room with four officers, two of whom were armed. Mr. Woody was one of the unarmed officers. When asked how he felt about Willie Grady, he stated that he "always felt uneasy" around him. He said that he noticed one day, while they were in the room waiting for the trial to begin, Cochran kept looking toward a window but never said anything. Woody was aware of his history of escapes, so he moved from where he was sitting to a long bench in front of the window. After that, Cochran never looked at the window again.

The un-airconditioned courtroom was packed with at least four hundred spectators. That many more waited outside. At that hour the July heat had not yet become oppressive. Courtroom windows were raised and ceiling fans turned slowly overhead.

Patricia's father and stepfather sat side by side in the courtroom, however, neither her mother nor Cochran's mother attended. In fact, no member of his family was present. Police officers from Floyd, Bartow and Paulding counties, as well as Georgia Bureau of Investigation agents, screened all spectators.

For the first time in Bartow County courthouse history, Judge Paschall allowed reporters and cameras in the courtroom. Paschall told reporters and photographers that they could move around and take any pictures they desired as long as they did not interfere with court proceedings.

When the case was called at nine o'clock, Cochran's lawyers made a motion for a continuance until the next term of court. The defense stated they had two grounds for a postponement. First, they felt that they had not had sufficient time to prepare as they had been appointed only two weeks prior. Secondly, they argued that public sentiment was too great against the defendant and that it was unsafe for him to stand trial at that time.

The prosecution objected to the motion and stated, "Counsel was appointed two weeks ago yesterday, and the State feels this is ample time to prepare for the defense."

Mitchell argued that the defense would have to show evidence that it was unsafe to try the case and that he felt Cochran could receive a fair trial.

Judge Paschall overruled the defense motion that they had not had sufficient time to prepare for trial. Regarding the second motion, he allowed the two young attorneys to present evidence showing public sentiment and excitement made it unsafe for Cochran to go on trial. The defense called Mr. M. L. Fleetwood to the stand.

"What is your business and profession, Mr. Fleetwood?" asked Corbitt.

"I am the Publisher of the *Daily Tribune News* and the *Weekly Tribune News.*"

The defense questioned the witness regarding photographs that had appeared in the Bartow County newspapers in recent weeks. Fleetwood admitted that his paper had published photographs of the victim's body immediately after it was taken from the river. He went on to admit that, not only were these photos published in the newspapers, but were displayed in the window of the newspaper office. The pictures were also made available for sale to the public.

It should be noted that in July of that year, Patricia's mother filed a damage suit in Bartow County. She sued the Tribune Publishing Company of Cartersville and M. L. Fleetwood, publisher of *Cartersville Tribune News*, asking for damages in the amount of twenty five thousand dollars for the newspaper's publication and sale of pictures taken of her daughter's body after it was recovered from the river. In her suit, she contended that the pictures were an invasion of her family's privacy and were published without the family's permission. Judge J. H. Paschall set the hearing for August and issued a temporary injunction against further display or sale of the photographs. Mrs. Waters eventually lost that suit when the Georgia Supreme Court ruled that the pictures were a matter of public record.

The prosecution objected to the pictures being entered into evidence and refused to view them. Judge Paschall ruled the pictures could not be entered into evidence.

The defense called a local businessman to the stand and attempted to show that prejudice existed toward the defendant, but the man stated, on cross examination, that he felt the jury could "do justice" on the case.

The Court denied the defense motion for a continuance.

At this point, the defense requested a plea of insanity be heard. The Judge agreed and a special jury was empanelled to hear the insanity plea.

Priscilla Sullins & Connie Baker

CHAPTER 13

The defense called Dr. Winston E. Burdine to the stand as its first witness.

Many people in the South (and other parts of the United States) had never heard of Sigmund Freud. But virtually everyone in the South had heard of Dr. Winston Burdine. Psychiatry was a relatively new field at that time. Anyone who felt a friend or relative needed to seek this type of professional help and wanted them to "see the best," sent them to Winston Burdine.

He received his B.S. from the University of Georgia, his D.S. of Medicine from Mercer University, and his Doctor of Medicine from the Medical College of Georgia. He had an internship at the Inglewood City Hospital in New Jersey and one at St. Anthony Hospital in Oklahoma City. He was a resident of Psychiatry at St. Elizabeth Hospital in Washington, D.C., a senior resident of Psychiatry in New Orleans, an instructor of Psychiatry at Louisiana State University School of Medicine and attended the

Washington School of Psychiatry for two years. His office was at the Medical Arts Building in Atlanta, Georgia.

The defense had retained his services, and Dr. Burdine had examined Cochran during the week before the trial.

Dr. Burdine testified at length about the tests and examinations that he and his associate, a licensed psychologist, performed. Over objections from the prosecution, he also voiced conclusions and diagnoses.

Burdine testified that, based on his examination, Cochran had a poor family background, rife with mental problems and heavy drinking. He stated Willie Grady felt his father was cruel and never gave him affection. Cochran thought his mother wasn't able to give him any warmth and that she nagged him.

Burdine stated, "He (Grady) got along with her (his mother) except when she nagged him; but apparently even though he has a great deal of hostility to her, he has been unable to break his ties with her."

Burdine spoke of Willie Grady's flat affect, his inappropriateness of response.

BURDINE: "His appearance was that of an individual with completely flat expression, by that I mean he didn't show any emotion at times when he should show emotion, for instance, when he was discussing killing this girl he showed very little emotion...he would have a blockage of speech, and he would suddenly come out with something that had no connection with the thing we were talking about; his predominating mood was one of sadness and depression; he was delusional at the time that I saw him, he felt that everyone was against him and that people picked on him in general; he was not hearing voices at that time, but he had stated that he heard God's voice on several occasions, and that at the time that he killed this little girl that God had told him to do it; he had heard other voices at times in the past, but he didn't know whose voice he heard."

As to right and wrong, Burdine had this to say, "I was of the opinion that there were times when this man knows right from wrong. I think the day I examined him, I asked him did he think he had done anything wrong and his first statement was 'That they say I have done something awful,' and I pinned him down and he indicated to me that he might think he had done something wrong by the fact that after he killed this girl he went back later to hide her. At the time he didn't think he had done anything wrong, but he went back later to take her body and hide it, which stated to me that he had realized at that time that he had done something wrong."

Dr. Burdine also made a diagnosis and prescribed treatment.

BURDINE: "I was of the opinion this was a case of schizophrenia of the paranoid type, and that his prognosis as for treatment and outlook is extremely poor. I felt that the only treatment that probably would be very helpful to him would be a prefrontal lobectomy, which is an operation they do on the area in the front of the brain, to cut down some of this hostility and some of this feeling that he has about other people."

Burdine offered this statement regarding motive, "Our psychological tests indicated that he had a great deal of hostility toward people in general, but especially so towards women, and I questioned him rather closely about his feelings towards females, and he said that they don't wear enough clothes. I associated this crime that he committed with the fact that the little girl had on a bathing suit, I am sure that that was the thing that upset him at the time."

BURDINE: "Based on my examination at that time, as to whether or not it is my opinion today if the defendant, William Grady Cochran, is sane or insane; well, I think he is insane."

There was objection from the prosecution, which was sustained.

Dr. Burdine was allowed by the court to give his definition of "a schizophrenic and psychopath" and to explain these disorders.

BURDINE: "The individual has difficulty in relating to other people; we find that throughout the lifetime of a schizophrenic he is unable to maintain proper inter-personal relationships with his family and friends and with other people; he is an individual who tends to withdraw from reality and live in a dream world of his own; he is an individual who may on one time become overly suspicious of everybody, usually they are more suspicious of those dearest to them emotionally; they are individuals who just never seem to get along, they may go off alone without any apparent reason; there are many of them that hear voices and even see visions. They may see the Lord or people that have been dead for two or three years. They more commonly hear the voice of God than anyone else, especially if they have any religious background at all; they have a lack of feeling for things that other people normally experience feeling for."

At this point Corbitt asked the key question.

CORBITT: "Dr. Burdine, state whether or not in your opinion, at the commission of this crime, allegedly on June 20, 1955, state whether in your opinion, this defendant, William Grady Cochran, was sane or insane at this time."

MITCHELL: "If the Court please, we object to that question as being immaterial and irrelevant."

THE COURT: "I sustain the objection."

CORBITT: "We, of course, Your Honor, think that..."

THE COURT: "I have already ruled on that, Mr. Corbitt, I sustain the objection."

CORBITT: "We want the record to show exception to that ruling."

THE COURT: "It is not necessary to show exceptions."

CORBITT: "Will you state whether or not, Dr. Burdine, it is your opinion this defendant, William Grady Cochran, was able to distinguish right from wrong today?"

MITCHELL: "If the Court please, we object to that question as being immaterial and irrelevant."

THE COURT: "I sustain the objection."

Having been effectively silenced on this issue, Corbitt sat down.

Mitchell began his cross-examination by questioning Dr. Burdine as to the amount of time he spent with Cochran, and if a psychologist performed any part of the examination.

Burdine testified that he went to Fulton Tower by himself, and that he questioned the defendant for about an hour on July 9th. He also stated that his associate had administered a test known as the T.A.T. He stated that this test was similar to the ink blot test in that the patient is shown pictures and interprets what he sees.

"For instance, you may have a picture of a boy playing the violin and his mother over-looking this boy...he (the patient) tells

You Can't Play Outside...

the story of what is happening. It is a little bit different from the inkblots, but they both serve the same purpose." He went on to relate that Cochran had described the picture of the boy playing the violin as "something about this mother being mean in making this boy practice."

Burdine said that Cochran was also given an intelligence test and scored in the average range. The doctor said that he examined the reports by his associate, but that he based his conclusions mainly on his interview with the defendant. Burdine testified that he had only seen Willie Grady that one time.

Burdine said that he based his knowledge of Cochran's family history not only from his interview with Willie Grady, but also from a welfare case study done in Floyd County. This study was completed when Cochran was transferred to Milledgeville from prison. It was done in Floyd County because his mother was living there at the time. Burdine explained that the welfare case study did not contain any medical records nor medical conclusions. He said that the study was completed by a lay worker giving background on the family.

Dr. Burdine further elaborated that he had never spoken with any other psychiatrist or medical doctor who had examined Cochran previously, nor with any of Cochran's family members, nor with any person who had known Willie Grady throughout his life.

The defense called Dr. Harvey Howell, a Bartow County physician. Corbitt attempted to have him testify concerning his opinion of Willie Grady based on reading Dr. Burdine's report. The prosecution strongly objected.

After arguments from both attorneys, the judge finally allowed the defense to pose a hypothetical situation to Dr. Howell and ask for his opinion.

The hypothetical situation assumed that Willie Grady Cochran's "mother was seventy years old and in poor health...that he liked her when she didn't nag at him...(that) his father had been dead about twenty years, he couldn't remember exactly how long; that he described his father as being mean, getting drunk a lot, beating him...that he was the fifth of seven children...that his father was in Milledgeville for some time, and that there were four or five uncles and aunts that had also been confined to Milledgeville; that he has never been able to adjust well to life, and he bases the fact that he hasn't on the premise that it is other people's fault and that they bother him...he leaves others alone unless the Lord tells him to bother them...he went through about the sixth grade...never married."

Corbitt went on to state that in the hypothetical situation, Willie Grady "states that he has hallucinations...neighbors were talking about him...he expresses hate for people in general and a special hate for women; that women, especially women in shorts and bathing suits upset him...he feels he is God's child."

CORBITT: "Dr. Howell, assuming that these facts are true and that they represent the medical history of this defendant, Willie Grady Cochran, will you tell the jury and the Court, in your opinion, today, whether or not this man is sane or insane?"

Howell testified that he didn't hear anything to make him think that the defendant was sane or insane. He stated that he could not attempt to give an opinion based solely on medical history, but would also need to talk to the defendant directly and observe his behavior. On cross-examination, he testified that he could not determine if the defendant was sane or insane. This testimony ended the defense's case.

CHAPTER 14

The prosecution called Bartow County Sheriff Frank C. Atwood as its first witness. Atwood testified that since the homicide of Patricia Ann Cook, he had had the opportunity to be with and speak with the defendant. He testified that prior to the homicide, he did not know Mr. Cochran personally but was acquainted with some of the Cochran family. Sheriff Atwood stated that he had spoken with Willie Grady during the ride to and from Fulton Tower in Atlanta. Mitchell asked Mr. Atwood's opinion of Cochran's intelligence and state of mind.

The defense objected to this question, saying this would call for the opinion of an expert.

The objection was overruled and Atwood was allowed to state, as a lay person, "that at the time we talked to him, he showed no evidence of being insane."

The second witness for the prosecution was Horace T. Clary, Major in the National Guard. Mr. Clary was allowed to give lengthy testimony regarding time spent with Willie Grady while he was in the Floyd County jail and about conversations he had with Cochran. He stated that the first time he saw Willie Grady Cochran was in the Floyd County jail. He said he was there, along with several other law enforcement personnel, trying to get Cochran to tell where the body of Patricia Ann Cook was located.

CLARY: "I went in and talked to Grady and at that time he told us that he would tell us where Patricia Ann's body was...we sat there and talked, and then we left to go to Milam's Bridge in Bartow County, where he had told us he could show us where the body was...On the drive to Milam Bridge, Sheriff Joe Adams was in the front seat and Mr. Brock was in the right front seat, and Grady and myself were in the back...without going into all the details...we stopped there and he pointed out the spot...we drove toward Atlanta slowly until we received the radio call that she had been found.

I was with him that day; well, it's hard for me to tell the exact time, I was rather nervous, we were all under strain, I would say four hours...but I talked to Grady at the jail, and, as I say, that is where he said he would show us the body. Grady was, I will say this, at that time, he was under emotional strain, as all of us were; when he told us that he would take us to the body, he seemed to relax all over; downstairs I talked to Grady and...he probably used better English than you or I in most of the conversation. He carried on a very lucid and sane conversation...

Grady did not want to talk too much about the crime, we stayed off of the crime, he just didn't want to tell, apparently, why; I was curious as to why the little girl had went with him and said something about a pistol that I had heard that he had bought or had...and he says, 'Yes, Major, I did,' and he said, 'I had it with me that day,'...and out of a complete blue to me he says, 'Major, I shot her'...I said, 'I'm glad to hear that, Grady, I'm glad the little girl didn't suffer by being choked'...Grady said, 'Major, I couldn't have choked the little girl.' I asked Grady where he hid the gun and he gave me exact directions where the gun was later found."

Clary went on to explain that as they drove to the Milam Bridge site, the National Guard had erected roadblocks at both ends of the bridge. It was later explained that they had put a National Guard jacket and helmet on Willie Grady to disguise him from the public as they walked him onto the bridge. Clary said that he remarked to Cochran that he thought the Guard had performed admirably and efficiently during the search and that he was proud of them.

CLARY: "Grady said, 'You ought to be proud of your men, Major,' I told him that I was awfully proud of my boys and Grady said, 'Major, I wish I was one of your boys.' Grady walked with me down on the bridge; I will say this, Grady told me that he would live up to his word and I could depend on his word, and I told him that he could depend upon my word also, and we got out, and I told him to come and go with me and he walked along by the side of me, and we walked, I will say, to the center of the bridge, and Grady had his head down and when we reached the spot he looked to the left, and, in my opinion, I am sure that he was counting the posts on the bridge, and then after he counted so much he took two steps forward and he said, 'Major, she is right there;' and then I asked him, I says, 'Now, Grady, how about the little girl's shoes, did you throw them in here?' he had told me that she would have on all of her clothes except her shoes, and he said, 'yes, sir, I threw them in there.' I said, 'Are you sure that chain is still on her?' I was still worried about the current, I was afraid that she might be floating, he said, 'Major she will be right there, that chain is on her.'"

Clary then related that he took Willie Grady back to the car, and along with the other officers began driving slowly toward Atlanta. They wanted to get Cochran out of the immediate area but were waiting to hear, via radio, if the body was found.

CLARY: "Grady realized that I was quite worried about whether it was the right place, and he told me, he said, 'Major, I am good for my word, she is there.' We drove along and he said, 'Major, they will find her before we reach Cartersville.' Well, they didn't, and the radio came on and wanted us to stop and call Rome to get some divers, and the person on the radio said that the water was eight or nine feet deep, as I recall, and Grady turned to me and apologized, because it had been more than ten minutes, and he said, 'I didn't know the water was that deep'...so we did stop and the Sheriff got out and made a phone call and called Rome...and as we went on towards Emerson the radio came on and said, 'we have found the little girl.' And when they had found her, of course, Grady turned to me and said, 'Major, I told you I was good for my word.'"

Clary testified that after they received word that Patricia's body had been found they drove on toward Atlanta. He testified that he spoke with Willie Grady about various subjects including Cochran's plan to purchase a refrigerated trailer and haul chickens to Atlanta or Chicago. Clary said that he thought Willie Grady was fond of his mother because that was one of the things that he asked for, along with his clothes. Clary had promised Willie Grady that he would bring him his clothes and bring his mother to visit him.

CLARY: "I had Mr. Brock, an officer, to go after his mother and his clothes, which I had promised him, but she would not go, because she was so upset and she said she would go down later, so I couldn't deliver on that promise...he told all of us that he was sorry for the trouble which he had caused...he said he wished there was some way that people like him could be stopped. Just before we got to Fulton Tower, he said, 'Well, all of you all can go home and get a good nights' sleep.' He even told me to come see him.

Certainly, in my opinion, any criminal...would have a warped or distorted mind...the way I look at it, but I certainly agree that he knows right from wrong, and I think Grady will admit that, that is just my opinion. In my general conversation about other things, as well as about the crime, as to whether or not he answered directly and forthrightly, or correctly; well, yes...I will say this, after we found the body, it came in on the radio, he turned to me and said, 'Major, you see, I am good for my word,' and I thanked him...As to whether he did anything or indicated by anything he said or did, that he felt that I, and all people, or any certain class of people were against him...well, I certainly don't think that he thought that about me; the reason I say that is that he requested that I go to Fulton Tower with him and stay with him at all times, and I did, and I asked him why he didn't tell—well, I think the Sheriff asked him first, Sheriff Adams, why didn't you tell me and he told the Sheriff, he said, 'Well Sheriff, I wanted to, but I just couldn't.' Certainly I don't think he had any animosity

You Can't Play Outside...

towards the Sheriff or myself, and Mr. Von Brock knew his mother very well, as I understood it, I think his mother was very close to Mr. Brock's family, and they seemed to be very friendly, and Deputy Sheriff Woody went down with us, and Lt. Varnadoe, and I thought we got along fairly well. Yes, he expressed to me that he was sorry for what he had done, several times; I will put it this way, I will correct it, he was sorry that he had caused us so much trouble; my job was to find the little girl, I was not the investigating officer, that was the Sheriff's job, but he was sorry for the trouble; Grady did not at any time wish to talk about anything he had done to the little girl other than he told me that he had shot her."

At this point the prosecution asked Mr. Clary to state, based on his conversations with Cochran and in his own opinion, whether Willie Grady was capable of assisting in his defense.

Corbitt objected that it would require an expert witness to make this opinion and that Clary was not qualified to answer.

Judge Paschall overruled the objection and allowed Clary to state that Willie Grady Cochran was legally sane.

A major issue during the sanity trial and during the ensuing murder trial was the fact that Willie Grady had been photographed with a black eye. Cochran stated to the press that he received the black eye in Rome. The defense endeavored to conclude that any confessions made by Cochran were under duress and were the result of a beating that occurred while he was being questioned in Floyd County.

CLARY: "The first time I saw this defendant was right after lunch on Saturday...he was in an upstairs cell at the Floyd County jail...at the time I first saw him his physical condition was apparently good, Grady was emotionally upset at the time I saw him. As to whether or not he evidenced any signs of a beating, whether he showed any marks on his face; well, no sir. I did see a picture in the paper that looked that way, but that picture was made several days before. I couldn't tell that there was anything wrong with him. As to whether or not he did not look as the picture represented, or whether I just did not notice; well, he looked much better than that picture did, yes sir...Grady will tell you that nobody touched him in my presence...

Of course, I don't claim any knowledge of psychiatry, and I am not going to tell this jury that I am speaking from the knowledge of psychiatry, that medically he is sane today; well, no sir, I am not a psychiatrist, I am speaking just of my opinion...yes, I know that Grady made previous statements to other officers that were not the truth...

What he said, finally, he said I looked like a man of my word, and he would show me where the little girl was. As to whether or not he at that time appeared to be afraid of the other officers, and was looking to me for security, whether or not I got that impression; well, Grady Cochran is not afraid of anything is this world, I will say that."

Then Clary testified that Willie Grady had mentioned to him that he had been in jail previously. Cochran said that he had been in trouble "along the same lines, but of course, never murder."

MITCHELL: "This other trouble you talk about, I will ask you whether or not he stated that he had served time for rape?"

CLARY: "He didn't state it in those words, but he knew that I knew that, and that he was speaking of that."

Corbitt objected on the grounds that this information would unduly prejudice the jury. Because the evidence had appeared in the Court, he asked for a mistrial. The judge overruled the objection and denied the motion for a mistrial. However, he did ask Mr. Mitchell how the information was material to the current trial. Mitchell argued that the information regarding the previous rape went to the question of motive.

Again Corbitt objected to the mention of the previous rape and again asked for a mistrial.

The judge denied the motion for a mistrial but told Mr. Mitchell, "You had better leave that out."

Mitchell asked that the jury be retired while he showed that his questioning was material to motive. The jury was retired and Mr. Mitchell began his argument.

MITCHELL: "But they are seeking and through their expert witness, Dr. Burdine, are seeking to show that he is insane; that the reason this crime was committed was because God told him to commit it. Now, I think we should have an opportunity to rebut that evidence; to show that he was not telling Dr. Burdine the truth, by showing a motive, why he killed her; that he has previously been sentenced to twenty years for the offense of rape; and will attempt to show by future introduction of evidence that he had intercourse, that he assaulted her on this occasion; that it would be perfectly logical for him to take her life because he had nothing to lose, and that would be a logical reason for the killing, rather than the illogical fact that God told him to, and to rebut what Dr. Burdine said he told him that he hated women."

Judge Paschall agreed with the prosecution and allowed the information of the previous rape conviction to remain. Mitchell went on to question Clary as to any conversations he had with the defendant relative to his sex life.

CLARY: "To the effect, I can't remember the exact words, that he had normal sex relations and he said he had two wives and two children, and had another woman pregnant at this time."

At no time was it ever brought into evidence, or otherwise alluded to, that Willie Grady Cochran had ever been married or fathered any children. In fact, Willie Grady was never married and never had children.

Mitchell recalled Sheriff Frank Atwood for further questioning. He was asked if Willie Grady had told him whether he had intercourse with Patricia Ann Cook.

Corbitt objected and was overruled.

ATWOOD: "He told us that he did have sexual intercourse with the little girl...as to what he stated after having intercourse with her he did; well, he said that he got the gun, I don't remember, I can't follow him just exactly right now, anyway, he went to the truck and got his gun and came back down into the woods where they were, and they were laying down upon the ground talking to one another, and he decided that he was going to have to kill her, and that he just pushed her over on her left side, and he shot down like this (indicating)."

Corbitt once again objected and made a motion for a mistrial, stating, "...the witnesses' evidence as to pushing her over and shooting her has no bearing on the question of insanity, and it could only prejudice the jury against this defendant."

Once again his motion was denied and his objection overruled.

The prosecution called Frank Clayton to the stand. Mr. Clayton identified himself as a parole supervisor, supervising twelve Northwest Georgia counties, including Paulding County, where Willie Grady Cochran resided. He testified that Cochran was a parolee under his supervision and that he began that supervision sometime in December of 1954. He stated that supervision included monthly reporting, days worked, and reasons for not working. Clayton said he had spoken with Cochran on several occasions since December 1954 in an official capacity.

CLAYTON: "I visited him at the saw mill...I did not have any trouble talking with him, or getting him to respond to any questions...he did not appear nervous or in any way out of the ordinary...

The last time I talked with him was on Tuesday morning...after this was supposed to have happened on Monday...he came to my house at Chatsworth...he told me that they was through sawing and that he was going to have to do something else, and he wanted to know if he could buy him a tractor and trailer and haul chickens from Gainesville...and he would be hauling meat and stuff like that back South; I stated to him that I thought those people hauled under contracts, and that, you know, he had better have a contract or something similar before he went into something like that...he wanted to see if he could do that, get permission before he bought the truck...that was the nature of our conversation. As to whether or not there was anything different insofar as his attitude or manner or faults; well, not that I could tell, no sir. Yes, this was Tuesday morning, I would say it was between eight and eight thirty...

On any of the times that I talked with this defendant, Grady Cochran, he never exhibited to me or said to me, or indicated to me in any way that he felt like that I and others were down on him, or that he was being persecuted."

Now the State called Dr. Thomas G. Peacock. Dr. Peacock stated that he was employed as superintendent of Milledgeville State Hospital, Milledgeville, Georgia, and that he was a licensed physician in the State of Georgia. He graduated from Harvard Medical School. He interned at Rochester General Hospital, Rochester, New York, and had seven years of private practice in

Hawkinsville, Georgia, and Thomaston, Georgia. He went to New Jersey State Hospital in 1929 and practiced there for ten years. He took courses in psychiatry, and practiced as a psychiatrist at New Hampshire State Hospital for two years and the Institute of Living in Hartford, Connecticut for three years. He returned South to Pine Bluff Sanitarium for two years and came to Milledgeville State Hospital in June 1947. He testified that he was a psychiatrist.

Peacock stated, in answer to questioning by Mitchell, that he had eleven thousand, six hundred and twelve inmates under his supervision at the state hospital in Milledgeville. He defined schizophrenia as the "splitting of the personality, it is a progress of mental illness, in as much as they...do not face reality, but seek refuge on the facts of life. The paranoid type of schizophrenia, as to what type that is; well, they have delusions of persecution and, at times, grandeur. Where there is a schizophrenic of the paranoid type with delusions of persecution, as to whether or not, in my opinion, he would communicate the fact that he felt he was persecuted to others, generally; well, they would."

Peacock stated that, in his opinion, a one-hour interview along with the tests described by Dr. Burdine, were not sufficient to make the diagnosis of paranoid schizophrenia. He stated that, in his practice, an observation of at least thirty days would be required to make a diagnosis. His opinion of the tests conducted by Dr. Burdine and the results was "that they were interesting, but not reliable."

Peacock further stated, "As to whether or not I have, myself, personally examined William Grady Cochran; well, so far as I can recall I have never seen him until today."

Corbitt began his cross-examination by questioning Dr. Peacock as to how many board certified psychiatrists were among the staff at Central State Hospital.

Peacock never gave a precise reply, but stated, "We have approximately forty doctors, I would say that several of them are eligible for the Board, we have one Board man, most of the doctors have been there over a year."

He stated that approximately twenty-five of the doctors had been there over a year and commented that he would rather have non-Board members than some Board members he had seen.

Peacock stated that Willie Grady Cochran had been sent to Milledgeville State Hospital from Tattnall Prison (the prison is located in Tattnall County and the county seat is Reidsville, Georgia) and that he was determined by the state hospital to be psychotic.

Peacock said that he had previously questioned whether a paranoid schizophrenic would "go up to the law enforcement officers or probation officers to tell them about their persecution complex and refuse to tell the doctors and friends; well, I think that the friends would probably know about it, the people they are more closely associated with, but they frequently do appeal to the law enforcement officers."

Peacock agreed that "there are any number of schizophrenics of the paranoid type walking the streets of Georgia today" and that it was one of the most difficult types of insanity to cure. He admitted that the tests used by Dr. Burdine were routinely used to support diagnoses. He stated that if he examined a patient and determined him to be suffering from a mental illness, but the tests did not agree with that diagnosis, "it wouldn't worry me one bit." He said if the tests did agree with his diagnosis, then "that would strengthen my examination and diagnosis...to a certain extent."

Mitchell began his re-direct of Dr. Peacock by questioning him regarding "persons who were feigning mental illness in order to avoid a trial in courts of law."

Peacock said, "Well, I wouldn't say how many, but I have had some experience...well, yes sir, it is often possible and very frequently happens that these patients give us false information...I have had patients that they (meaning Tattnall prison administrators) sent in to us, they (the inmates) would intimate, but I may be a little bit prejudiced along that line, but I do know that many of them feign mental illness to get up to the state hospital where they say the food is better, I don't know that it's true. Mr. Balkum (warden) would probably disagree with me, but they say so, and it is easier to escape from the Milledgeville State Hospital."

Peacock said that Cochran was sent to the state hospital by the Board of Corrections, upon the recommendation of the State Psychiatric Board. He emphasized that a judge did not send Cochran there. Cochran was admitted on September 21, 1948, and was discharged on February 14, 1950.

He said that the staff at Milledgeville determined "that if he had psychosis it was due to the taking of excessive amounts of Benzedrine, but at the time that he appeared before the Board, it was determined that he should be returned to Tattnall Prison."

Now the defense began a re-cross examination. Peacock testified that Cochran's history mentioned a birth injury and that, if the history was true, a birth injury "could result in a degree to a mental disability or psychotic condition or insanity." He was questioned again about the cure rate of paranoid schizophrenics. Peacock again stated that the staff's determination was that Cochran was not psychotic when he was returned to Tattnall Prison. He stated that he read Cochran's medical history and could only find one mention of Cochran saying that he was afraid of other inmates. He said this was noted only in the welfare history, and Cochran was not diagnosed as paranoid at Milledgeville.

On re-direct by Mitchell, Peacock said "he (Cochran) could have a normal fear of being injured by another inmate...persons tell me that it is a real fear that is not based on delusions or hallucinations."

Peacock reiterated that the welfare report was information furnished by Cochran's mother and obtained by a social worker sending out a questionnaire. The report was not completed by a psychiatrist or doctor. He stated that there were six doctors on the Board that determined to send Cochran back to Tattnall Prison.

On re-cross by Corbitt, Dr. Peacock stated, "As to whether or not, unfortunately, we do make mistakes down at Milledgeville in releasing patients at times; well, we do."

The State rested its case here, and the defense re-called Dr. Burdine. Burdine testified that he accepted employment from the defense on the condition that a report of his examination be sent to both the defense and the Court. He stated that his report was sent to the Solicitor. Dr. Burdine reiterated that, in his opinion, paranoid schizophrenia could not be easily cured and that symptoms could recur and/or remain for a period of time. He stated that he knew of no way to determine if or when these symptoms would or could recur.

When Burdine finished this testimony, the evidence was closed and the jury was charged.

The charge from Judge Paschall included, "A person shall be considered of sound mind who is neither an idiot, a lunatic, nor afflicted with insanity, and who has arrived at the age of fourteen years, or before that age, if such person know the distinction between good and evil...no lunatic or person afflicted with insanity shall be tried, or put upon his trial, for any offense during the time he is afflicted with such lunacy or insanity."

The jury was charged to find in favor of the special plea of insanity or to find against the special plea of insanity.

It was now past noon and the heat in the courtroom was becoming more noticeable as the jury was recessed for lunch. They began deliberations on the insanity issue and returned their verdict around two o'clock.

The jury found against the special plea of insanity.

Judge Paschall dismissed them and called for a ten-minute recess.

You Can't Play Outside...

CHAPTER 15

At two forty-five the selection of jurors to hear the murder case began. The jury consisted of eleven men and one woman. All were white and the woman's occupation was listed as housewife and businesswoman. The men selected included four merchants, a miner, a garage parts man, a mechanic, a shoe repairman, a carpenter and two farmers.

At four o'clock the murder case was called. The ceiling fans were no longer effective against the southern, July heat. As everyone anticipated the beginning of testimony, Judge Paschall called for silence. Only the whirring of the fans and the sounds of insects hitting the screens of the open windows could be heard.

Despite the sweltering heat, no spectators left the courtroom.

White and Corbitt, having shed their suit jackets, their starched dress shirts wilting, again asked for a postponement. Denied.

The first witness for the State was John D. Cook, Patricia's father. He testified that he was her father and gave her age at the time of her death.

Patricia's stepfather, J.C. Waters, was called next. Mr. Waters testified that Patricia was missing when he came home from work and that he and her mother were unable to locate her after searching and making telephone calls to friends and neighbors. He stated that his wife was unable to be in the courtroom because she was under a doctor's care. When Mitchell completed his questions, the defense did not cross-examine.

Mrs. Evelyn Johnson was called by the State. She testified regarding her conversation with Willie Grady Cochran at two o'clock on Monday, June 20th. She said that he had asked her if she knew where he could find a girl to do some work for him.

Again there was no cross-examination and Mrs. Jane Kinsey was called to the stand. She identified Cochran as the man who came to her house on East Nineteenth Street at sometime after two o'clock on Monday, June 20th. She stated that he asked her if she knew a family named Crawford and that he left in a light colored pick up truck. The defense did not cross-examine Mrs. Kinsey.

The next witness for the state, Myrtle Scoggins, gave her address as East Nineteenth Street. She stated that she saw Patricia Ann Cook pass by her house in the passenger seat of a light colored pick up truck sometime in the afternoon of Monday, June 20th. She did not see the driver of the truck. The defense chose not to cross-examine this witness.

Mr. H. H. Duncan was called to testify by the State. He said he owned a grocery store and that the store, just inside the Bartow County line, was built onto his living quarters. He identified Willie Grady Cochran as the man who came to his store on Monday, June 20th at about six thirty or seven o'clock in the evening. According to Duncan, Cochran drove up to the store and blew the horn. He was in a gray-green pick up truck and he asked for two Double Colas. When Duncan brought the drinks out to the truck, he saw a little girl on the passenger side.

He testified that, "Well, she just looked like she was mashed up in the corner of the truck, just as far as she could get, I never saw her move or bat her eyes, or nothing."

On cross-examination, Corbitt asked which way the man went when he left the store. Duncan stated that the truck was headed towards Cartersville but that he never actually saw which way the truck went when Cochran left.

On re-direct, the prosecutor asked about the girl's identity. Duncan stated that he was shown a picture of Patricia Ann Cook, and that he had identified her as the girl in the truck with Cochran.

The next witness called by the State was Mrs. H. H. Duncan, wife of the previous witness. She corroborated her husband's testimony and added her encounter with Cochran and especially with Patricia.

"I seen a little girl sittin' in there with him, sittin' just as straight up as she could sit,...and her eyes looked awful to me. As to what I mean by her eyes looked awful to me, well, they looked hot, they looked like hot glass, and she just wiggled her fingers at me...like she wanted to tell me something, and I stood there and looked at her,...I wanted to go to her, out there, ask her was there something she wanted; so, I stood there and looked at her a little bit more, she just kept wiggling her fingers like that (indicating with her hand up and backwards, almost like she was beckoning), and I walked out in the yard where the truck was at, and I asked him was there anything else they wanted, he said, 'No, he is waiting on us,' (meaning her husband was getting the drinks) so I walked back in on the porch and turned around and looked back at her and she was still wiggling her fingers at me."

Mrs. Duncan identified Cochran as the man she saw on June 20th, and said she had seen a photograph of Patricia Ann Cook and identified her as the girl in the truck that day. She answered Corbitt's cross-examination question that the truck came from the Rome direction.

The State called Lillian Dempsey, of Stilesboro, Georgia, in Bartow County. Mrs. Dempsey testified that a man she identified as Cochran came by her store late in the afternoon of June 20th, driving a light colored pick up truck. She said she was sitting on her porch and that her store was right next to her house. When she went to the store to wait on the man, she noticed a young girl in the truck and the girl stared at her as she walked from her porch to the store.

"I could see her, and just thought that she was staring at me, and it kindly got me, because I didn't know what she meant by staring at me like that."

Mrs. Dempsey stated the man asked for three soft drinks, paid her and left in the direction of Cartersville, away from Rome. She thought it was around seven or eight o'clock in the afternoon when this occurred, but could not be sure.

Next on the stand for the State was George Fowler. Mr. Fowler testified that he had lived in the Burnt Hickory section of Paulding County all his life. He stated that he was acquainted with Willie Grady Cochran and that on June 20th, he was visiting at the home of Cochran's brother. He said it was late in the afternoon when he saw Willie Grady sixty to seventy feet from him. Willie Grady was cutting off a piece of baling wire that was in the yard. He testified that Cochran's brother called out and asked him what he was doing.

According to Fowler, Willie Grady said, "I was just getting a piece of wire, I am going down here for awhile. I will see you after a while."

He said Willie Grady left after that and he did not see him again.

Mitchell called Rome Detective Bill Terhune to the stand. Terhune stated that he participated in the investigation of the homicide of Patricia Ann Cook and that he was present at Cochran's arrest. Terhune was with Cochran when he showed officers the place on Old Lucus Road where he parked with Patricia.

Corbitt interrupted the testimony when Terhune began to state what Cochran had told him.

Judge Paschall had the jury go to the jury room while he and the attorneys discussed what Terhune would be allowed to say. Corbitt did not want any testimony of statements made by Cochran allowed unless it was first shown that the statements were freely and voluntarily given.

Mitchell argued that although any confession not freely and voluntarily given would not be admissible, any evidence adduced from a confession not freely and voluntarily given would be admissible.

You Can't Play Outside...

It might be noted that although Willie Grady Cochran had basically given a full confession of the kidnapping and murder of Patricia Ann Cook, he had refused to sign any written document.

Judge Paschall opined that although he would not allow any confession that was not freely and voluntarily given, statements made by the defendant might be different. Mitchell said that, in order to remove any question, he would remove the current witness and substitute another witness to the confession, E. M. Whitfield.

Corbitt wanted the question settled immediately as it would inevitably come up with other witnesses, but Judge Paschall took a "wait and see" stance and called the jury back.

The State then called GBI Agent E. M. Whitfield to the stand. Whitfield testified that Willie Grady Cochran gave him a statement as to the alleged offense.

Whitfield further stated, "At the time that this statement was made, as to whether any inducement was given to him whatsoever, none, sir. There were not any promises of reward made to him, or any hope of benefit held out to this defendant. Yes, he was advised of his rights. As to what he was advised; well, he was advised by yourself, sir, of his right to counsel, and anything he said might be used against him, and that he did not have to make any statement to us if he did not desire to do so. Yes, after being so advised, he did make a statement."

At this time Corbitt asked to cross-examine the witness. He asked if Whitfield had been present at the arrest of Willie Grady Cochran, to which he answered that he had not. Corbitt asked if the agent knew of any threats made to Cochran prior to his questioning of him on June 27th. Whitfield denied knowledge of any threats made to the defendant, either at the time of the statement or any previous time.

Corbitt objected to the testimony of Whitfield, as it could not be established that Whitfield would have known about previous threats.

The judge overruled the objection and the testimony continued.

E. M. Whitfield testified that Willie Grady Cochran made a confession to him in the presence of other law enforcement officers at the Bartow County Jail on June 27th, 1955. He stated that Cochran told him that he went to Rome early on June 20th, to see his brother at the county prison. Cochran said he left there and went to Milner Motors to have his brother's truck put in his name. He also went to see a relative in Lindale and to an unnamed place and drank a beer.

According to Whitfield, Cochran stated he was looking for a boy named Sims, who lived on East Nineteenth Street and owed him twenty dollars. He told Whitfield that he stopped at two or three places trying to find Sims. He came to a house and asked the girl who came to the door if she knew Sims and she replied that she did not.

Whitfield said Cochran told him, "We got to talking, and I said, 'You ought to be in swimming.' She had on a bathing suit; we talked about it being hot, and I said, 'I'd like to be in swimming myself.' She asked me if I was going to a swimming pool, and I said, 'I could.' She got a robe and put it on and we got in the truck, my truck, and I drove to a swimming pool at Roy's place and stopped there, and I said, 'Do you want to go in swimming?' She said, 'I can't swim.' I asked if she wanted to go riding and she said that she would not mind, but that she had to get back and cook supper."

Cochran told Whitfield that he rode out Chulio Road and crossed over into Bartow County, where he stopped to get some drinks. He left there and rode on up to Dempsey's Place to get more drinks. When he left the store he crossed the railroad and went to Taylorsville Highway. From there he turned onto Old Lucus Road, stopped and stayed a few minutes. He drove further up the road and stopped again. Cochran and the girl got out and went about thirty feet from the truck into the woods and lay down.

Cochran told Whitfield that she pulled her bathing suit off, and he didn't force her to have intercourse with him, "but we had one." She put her suit back on and they sat on the ground and talked, staying there about an hour and a half.

Whitfield testified that Cochran said, "I went up to the truck and got my gun, a .38 revolver, put it in my pocket and went down to where Patricia Ann Cook was lying, she had told me what her name was; we sat there and she wanted to know what I was going to do with the gun, if I was going to shoot her; I said, 'I don't know.' I didn't want her to know that I was, I knew I was, that is why I went and got the gun; she was lying on the ground, and she rolled over and turned on her back, turned her back to me, I shot her then; I made sure she was dead; I didn't want her to suffer, I just meant to kill her; I left her there and got in my pickup and went down the Lucus Road to Georgia 53...went to Cartersville and to home, stayed about one hour."

Whitfield's testimony continued with Cochran's description of his return to the Old Lucus Road. He gave Cochran's account of wrapping the body and dropping it into the river.

He further told Whitfield that he hid the pistol Wednesday morning in the barn.

Corbitt spoke up, "May it please the Court, at this time we would like to make a motion for a mistrial on the grounds that his confession has gone before the jury, without, we think, the proper showing being made, or the defendant being given the chance to show that this confession was not freely and voluntarily made, and it is impossible to take the impression of this confession from the minds of the jury, and I move for a mistrial at this time."

The Court overruled his motion.

Whitfield continued his testimony. He stated that Willie Grady Cochran showed him, along with other law enforcement officers, where he took Patricia Ann and also the route that they drove that day.

At the conclusion of Whitfield's testimony, Mitchell recalled Detective Terhune to the stand to give the date (June 24th) that he went with Willie Grady Cochran to the Old Lucus Road.

Since it was near five p.m., Judge Paschall recessed court for the day. The prosecution would continue its case the following morning.

Cochran was led from the courtroom surrounded by deputies and taken back to Atlanta.

Priscilla Sullins & Connie Baker

CHAPTER 16

At 9:00 a.m. on July 15th, the second day of the murder trial began. Once again the courtroom was filled to capacity.

Horace T. Clary was sworn in as the prosecution's first witness. Mr. Clary stated that he was an attorney, the Assistant Solicitor of the Rome Judicial Circuit, and a Major in the 2nd Battalion of the 122nd Infantry of the Georgia National Guard. He stated that he was in command of the Georgia National Guard unit that assisted in the search for the body of Patricia Ann Cook. He said that he had occasion to talk with Willie Grady Cochran on Saturday afternoon, following the Monday of Patricia's disappearance. The Guard had searched from Wednesday night until that Saturday at noon, and they had searched three or four locations pointed out by the suspect, Willie Grady Cochran.

Corbitt once again asked that his objection to the admissibility of the statements be recorded.

Clary continued his testimony, saying that he was prevailed upon to talk to Cochran at the Floyd County jail. He stated that

Detective Terhune and Chief Brock took him to Cochran's cell on the top floor. After they entered the cell, he asked both men to leave.

Clary said, "I was looking at Grady. I talked to Grady about what my job was, I told him that I had really only one purpose and that was to find the body of Patricia Ann Cook, and second is, if the body was found to protect him, if the need arose, and that I wanted him to point out where the body was."

Clary said he told Cochran that Patricia's mother was hospitalized and that Cochran's own mother was emotionally distressed and that he "should have a heart and see that the little girl was given a decent burial." He said that Cochran would cry but would not say where the child's body was.

Corbitt objected again to testimony of the defendant's statements without proof that they were freely and voluntarily given. Judge Paschall told the witness to show whether the statements were freely and voluntarily given.

CLARY: "I made no threats of bodily harm; nor did I make any promise of leniency, there was no promise of leniency made at all. I did...when he told me he would show me where the body was, (tell him that) I would do certain things, such as seeing his mother and all. I did tell him that I would see that that was done. No sir, there was no inducement made to him whatsoever, nor were there promises of benefits held out to him, unless seeing his mother and getting his clothes to him, no sir; so far as any benefit of the charge that he was under, no sir, that was not discussed."

When Corbitt began his cross-examination, Clary stated that Saturday morning was the first time he had ever seen or talked to Cochran and that he did not see any evidence of a beating. He had seen the picture in the paper showing Cochran with a black eye, but did not see any evidence of that. He also stated that Cochran was "visibly upset emotionally." Corbitt continued to question Clary regarding signs of a beating and Clary continued to deny any knowledge of it and stated again that he did not see any evidence of a beating when he spoke with Cochran.

Mitchell began his re-direct and Clary related what Cochran had told him. Clary said that he was afraid that Patricia Ann might still be alive and abandoned somewhere and he told

Cochran this fear. Cochran told him, "No, Major, she is not alive, she is dead." Clary reiterated that Cochran was in an extremely emotional state. Cochran said, "Why did I do it?" to which Clary replied, "Grady, I don't know why you did it, you are sick."

Clary said that Cochran wanted to see his mother and that he told him, "Grady, I have looked in the Etowah River, my men are exhausted. I have got good men, I have looked all over the mountains out on Lucus Road,...they are exhausted and given out, I says, I want to know where she is now, I want the point pointed out to us and then you can see your mother."

Clary told Cochran that he would take him back to Fulton Tower after he showed him where the body was. Clary said that Cochran told him, "Major, you just look like you are a man of your word, I will show you where she is."

Corbitt renewed his objection and argued that Cochran was promised to be taken to Fulton Tower and to be able to see his mother in return for showing where the body was. Corbitt said this was quite an inducement, and that the testimony should be inadmissible.

After argument of counsel, the Court allowed the testimony and Mr. Clary continued with his story.

Clary related that Cochran told him that he had put her in the river. When he asked Cochran how he knew she would still be where he put her, Cochran said he had weighted the body down with a heavy wrench and chain. Clary testified that, at that point, Cochran asked him to get fifty-five dollars that was allegedly taken from him when he was arrested and to keep photographers from taking his picture. Clary agreed to both.

Defense counsel again objected and stated that these were inducements, but was once again overruled by the Court.

Clary continued his testimony and said that Cochran told him, in the presence of other police officers, "I will give you my word, Major, that is where she is, and I will point out exactly where she is." Clary said that he, Cochran and two other police officers got in the car and headed to the Milam Bridge in Bartow County. He stated that Cochran was given a National Guard jacket and helmet to wear so no one would recognize him, and that no pictures were taken of Cochran as they left the Floyd County Jail.

Relating the account of the conversation in the car as they drove to Bartow County, Clary told Cochran that he had heard he had a gun. Cochran admitted to having one with him on the day of the kidnapping and murder. Clary was totally surprised when, "out of the blue," Cochran said that he shot Patricia. Officers were dispatched to look for the gun where Cochran said he had hidden it.

Clary testified that Cochran was very cooperative during the ride and when they reached the bridge, Cochran walked along side of him to the center of the bridge, pointed to a spot and said that she would be there. He told Clary that she would be found before they reached Cartersville. As they neared the outskirts of town, they were radioed that the water was over nine feet deep and divers were needed. Cochran said he didn't know it was that deep. Divers were called and the car with Cochran and the officers moved toward Atlanta.

They then received another radio call, "We have found the little girl." According to Clary's testimony, Cochran said, "Major, I told you I was good for my word."

Corbitt asked Clary why they disguised Cochran and intimated that perhaps they were worried about mob violence. Clary stated he did not think about that or consider it as a factor, that he took precautions because he felt responsible for him. He said he took Cochran to Fulton Tower as he had promised and that he felt like Cochran had been under a tremendous mental strain and just wanted to rest.

CLARY: "I don't know whether he, himself, was afraid of any mob violence being directed at him; well, you have asked me something that I want to say, and I am telling it to him, I don't believe Grady Cochran is scared of anything in this world."

The State next called Herman Evans to the stand. Mr. Evans was a Floyd County policeman. He testified that he found the gun at Cochran's mother's house exactly where Cochran said it would be. He identified the gun and stated that it was loaded when he found it.

Sheriff Frank Atwood testified next. As he began to tell about his conversation with Willie Grady, Corbitt objected and asked that it be shown that his client had made the statements without threats or promises. Sheriff Atwood said that Willie Grady had been apprised of his rights and that no threats or promises were made. He testified that he had seen Cochran on Wednesday night at the jail in Rome and that Cochran did not show any signs of a beating at that time. He next saw Cochran on Monday, the day of the confession, and again on the following Wednesday when Corbitt and White were appointed as Cochran's lawyers.

Atwood admitted that on the following Monday when he saw Cochran, "Well, he had evidence of a dark eye, the right one. Yes, his face was bruised up on that side...Yes, I had him sent to Fulton Tower in Atlanta. As to whether or not I had him sent down there because of fear of the possibility of mob violence; well, I figured it would be for our protection in this county because you never know what might happen in these cases, I just always feel better to have the prisoner secured. As to whether or not I felt like it would be better for Grady's safety if he was confined in Fulton Tower, in Atlanta; well, this is the way I felt about it, yes sir."

Atwood went on to tell about Cochran taking him and other officers to the site of the murder. He said that the Old Lucus Road was a "very old saw mill road" and that it was very rough. Cochran looked carefully around the area before he pointed out the exact site, and Atwood estimated that the site was about three miles "as the crow flies" from Cochran's home in Paulding County. He told basically the same story as Terhune and Whitfield. Cochran had told them that he had intercourse with Patricia, that she turned on her left side and that he shot her in the back.

Sheriff Atwood testified that he was present when Cochran pointed out the spot on the bridge where he threw the body and that he was also present when the body was recovered. He said that Carl Green and Herman Evans were in the boat when they found the body.

ATWOOD: "Yes, I saw the body there on the bank. As to what the condition was; well, she was wrapped completely in this quilt, her feet were showing and the top of her head was showing a little bit, her hair...The body was taken from the river to the funeral home. I also saw the body there at the funeral home. It was in the same condition as far as being wrapped, in the same condition as it was when it was brought from the river...It was in the same condition when they began their autopsy as it was when it was brought from the river, so far as being wrapped."

Atwood then looked at a photograph taken at the funeral home and stated that it reflected the condition that he had observed.

Corbitt cross examined the sheriff as to where the actual Bartow County line was in that area and the sheriff stated he could not put his hand on the actual line, but that he knew the spot that Cochran had shown them was in Bartow County.

Corbitt objected then on the grounds that it had not been proven the crime occurred in Bartow County.

Judge Paschall again overruled him.

Nancy Jones took the stand to testify that she had identified the body as that of Patricia Ann Cook.

The State called Dr. Herman D. Jones. Dr. Jones lived in Atlanta and was the director of the Georgia Crime Laboratory. He gave his considerable credentials which included a medical degree from Vanderbilt University in Nashville, Tennessee, a professorship at Auburn University in Alabama and at Oglethorpe University in Atlanta, Georgia, and an association with the Alabama Toxicological Laboratory. Immediately prior to his current position, he was director of the Fulton County Scientific Crime Laboratory in Atlanta.

Jones stated that on June 25th, he came to Bartow County, at the request of Sheriff Atwood to perform an autopsy on the body of Patricia Ann Cook.

JONES: "When I arrived, the body was at the Owen Funeral Home, in Cartersville. As to what the condition of the body was at that time, as to any clothing or other material around the body; well, when I first saw the body it was still on the ambulance cot, in the zipper bag, the zipper at the time I saw it was about half way down, in other words, a part of the chest and head was exposed when I first saw it; we pulled the zipper completely open then; from about the chin to the top of the head was exposed, from there down the body was wrapped in the thick heavy piece-quilted quilt, the heavy chain wrapped around the waist, attached to the chain on the right side was the large stilsen wrench. The photograph which you tender to me, marked for identification as State's

Exhibit Number Four, I can identify that photograph positively. As to how that photograph compares with the condition of the body at the time that I first saw it at the funeral home; well, that is the condition as I first saw it after we had taken it from the zipper bag, yes sir."

As Mitchell was asking the doctor to point out specifics on the photograph, Corbitt objected to the picture being submitted on the grounds that it "can only tend to prejudice the jury...it is a highly inflammatory picture."

The Court overruled.

Dr. Jones continued his testimony of the condition of the body and the position of the chain and wrench.

JONES: "It (the wrench) was on the right side of the body, and the first observation I made was the chain going up the back and around the neck, and further inspection of the body showed that the chain was wrapped around the waist five times, and was wired together with baling wire on the right side, with the wire going through the links of the chain, and then a link of the end hook, tied to that same piece of baling wire was this stilsen wrench, and it was wrapped twice, there was two strands of wire around the wrench, and then again twisted together; as I followed the chain up to the neck, there was only one wrapping of the chain around the neck, that was pulled pretty tight, the chain around the waist was not too tight, it was loose, you could move the chain backwards, but the chain around the neck was tight enough that to move it you have to put a little pressure on it; now, on the end of that chain around the neck there was baling wire through the link of the chain and then to the hook at the end of the wire. The next observation was the way the quilt was fastened around the ankles, one loop of wire around the ankle and then a loop of wire threaded through the quilt...the wire protruding up over this white background. There is two ends of quilt tied together by threading the wire through and pulling it together as you can observe from the photograph there, fairly tight around the legs."

Jones identified another photograph showing the things he removed from the body: the quilt, the beach coat, the chain, the wire, the Stillson wrench and the bathing suit.

The doctor testified that the cause of death was traumatic injury of the heart, with excessive bleeding. "...after removing the chain and lifting the quilt we next observed the beach coat...the faded red bathing suit was observed. By slipping the front of the bathing suit open slightly we observed a large wound in the left chest, and then observing the bathing suit, there was a hole in the front of the left side of the bathing suit; the bathing suit was then slipped off, and on examining the back of the body, a smaller wound was observed; the wound in the back was round; it was one-fourth inch by one-fourth inch...the wound in the front was more oblong..."

Jones identified a photograph of the wounds and stated that the wound on the back of the body was the bullet's point of entry. He testified that he found evidence of anti-mortem or pre-death bruising at the base of the neck or what is commonly called the Adam's apple and more severe bruising in front of the left shoulder, just under the collar bone.

Mitchell then asked the doctor if he found evidence of male sperm and Jones replied that he had.

Corbitt objected to this, saying that any proof would be immaterial and irrelevant and that it would be prejudicial to his client, and the Court overruled.

Dr. Jones said that he had requested that the autopsy room be cleared before he took a vaginal smear. He presented a photograph of the results of that test, and stated that the examination showed the presence of male sperm.

Mr. Corbitt again objected and was again overruled.

The State then began to bring into evidence certain articles and to have them identified by Dr. Jones. These included the bathing suit, beach coat, quilt, chain, wrench, and wire. When these items were presented, Patricia's father and stepfather averted their eyes.

Corbitt's objections that these articles "would be highly prejudicial to this defendant" were overruled.

Jones identified the articles and they were entered into evidence. He said that the beach coat had been completely buttoned and that there was a hole in both the beach jacket and the front of the bathing suit. These holes, he said, were consistent

You Can't Play Outside...

with the wound on her body, indicating that she was wearing them at the time she was shot.

When it was Corbitt's turn to cross-examine the witness, he asked if and when Dr. Jones had ever seen Willie Grady Cochran.

JONES: "Well, the first and only time that I have ever seen him was Wednesday night, June 22nd, in Rome—let me qualify that, with the exception then on Monday when he was brought down to the laboratory, making the two times that I have seen him. Yes, I examined him on the night in question. As to whether or not I observed any signs of physical beating or anything of the sort; well, not that I could see that night, no sir. As to whether or not he had a black eye or any bruises on his face; well, not that I saw. As to the time that I examined him on the following Monday down at my laboratory...well, no, I didn't examine him then...I didn't speak to him or ask him any questions, and he didn't speak to me; I brought this material out and placed it in front of him, and the solicitor questioned him...I had nothing to do with that...I didn't really observe him at all...they didn't ask me to examine him, and I did not. As to whether or not I didn't observe any bruises or a black eye at that time; well, no, I wasn't even thinking about it; they didn't request it and I didn't make any examination whatsoever...I just try to do what is requested of me and leave it at that. On the Monday examination, I won't say whether or not he had these bruises or did not have them."

Mitchell re-directed the examination by asking the doctor to say that he had heard Cochran's responses to Mitchell's questions to Cochran regarding the articles just brought in evidence. Jones stated that Willie Grady had, in his presence, identified the quilt, wrench, chain and baling wire as things that belonged to him or that he had gotten from his home. He said that Cochran also identified the beach coat and bathing suit as the clothes worn by Patricia Ann Cook.

The State called Jake Kiser of East Seventh Street, Rome, Georgia. Kiser testified that he had seen Cochran on the morning of June 20th and that Cochran had been parked across the street from his house in a Ford pick-up truck. He stated that he went in and out of his house several times and that his four daughters followed him several times. Cochran never got out of the truck while he was home and the truck was still there when he left his house. He was questioned as to what his oldest daughter was wearing and he said that she had on shorts.

Mary Kiser was next to testify. She said after her father left, that the man in the truck came to the door and asked her if she knew a Mrs. Crawford. She told him that she didn't and went to ask her mother next door. When she came back and told him that her mother did not know a Mrs. Crawford, either, "he just kept standing there staring at me, and he looked down at my legs." Mary Kiser said that she then turned around and went back into the house. The screen door to her house was locked and Cochran stood on the steps for about ten minutes before leaving.

When the Kisers' testimony was completed the State rested its case. It was 11:15 a.m. when the defense called Dr. Winston Burdine to the stand.

CHAPTER 17

Dr. Burdine's testimony was much the same as his testimony during the insanity hearing. He gave his credentials and explained that he went over tests given to Cochran by a psychologist and also read various histories and medical and psychiatric files on the defendant.

He stated that he interviewed Willie Grady Cochran in Fulton Tower. He found that "...his history, beginning as a child...was unable to adapt well with other people; he had difficulty in his relationships with members of his family, and on into school he was just an individual who just didn't seem to fit into his niche of society...he was the child of a father who was a rather...sadistic individual...as the prisoner described, never did anything nice for him...his mother...was unable to show a great deal of warmth and affection to him; and in school he had some difficulty in adjusting to the teachers and with the other students; after he quit school his occupational history was extremely poor...several times he had fairly good jobs, but was never able to hold onto a job, he didn't seem to fit in there; his anti-social record is an extremely long one...he has a history of being arrested probably as much as a hundred times, for all types of things...a history of spending many years in prison...somewhere close to fifteen years...while in prison he had a great deal of difficulty adjusting."

Burdine testified that Cochran was committed to the state mental hospital at Milledgeville for eighteen months while serving time at Reidsville Prison, and that there was a record of attempted suicide at Reidsville. He said that the psychological exam showed "a certain amount of hostility toward the opposite sex" and that he noted in Cochran's record a mention of a birth injury. Burdine felt that Cochran suffered from paranoid schizophrenia and described it as a "Dr. Jekyll and Mr. Hyde" syndrome. He noted Cochran's flat affect and also the fact that he heard voices from God. He gave a lengthy explanation of schizophrenia and the inkblot tests that were given to Cochran.

BURDINE: "Yes, he told me about the alleged crime...well, the way that he told me the story is that he picked this little girl up and carried her to the swimming pool,...he asked her if she would like to get out, and he said she said, 'no.' They drove off and he told me that she remarked to him that he reminded her of her daddy...he was a little bit reluctant to tell me about killing her, I had to question him at length about what happened and how it happened. He finally told me that he shot her in the back, and I asked him did he leave immediately, and he said, 'no.' He was unable to leave because she was still alive, and I asked him what he did, and he said that he held her head in his lap until she died, and to me that indicated something abnormal, for an individual to kill someone in cold blood, without any qualms about it, and then, yet, at the same time feel enough tenderness and passion about the thing to stay there and hold her head until she died. I said, 'Well, why did you kill her?' He said, 'Well, God kept telling me to,' and he went on to mention the fact about bathing suits and people, or women, not wearing enough clothes and how that was bad; and when he left there, apparently, he still was not sure that he had done anything wrong, but some little time after he left...it must have come to him that he had done something wrong, because he turned around and went back and got her and hid her body up until he made the decision to go back. I think he was probably acting under a psychotic impulse, but he certainly must have begun to realize he had done something wrong or he wouldn't have attempted to go back."

Burdine stated he thought that Cochran was delusional and was hallucinating the voice of God at the time of the murder, but that he could not say for sure if he thought Cochran knew right from wrong at the time. Burdine said that, in his opinion, Willie Grady Cochran was insane.

Mitchell brought up some of the same things in his cross-examination as he did during the insanity phase of the trial. He questioned the validity of the tests and also whether the doctor could tell when a patient was malingering. His cross-examination was extensive but he could not shake Burdine's opinion that Willie Grady Cochran was insane.

Burdine's testimony had been lengthy and Paschall called a recess for lunch.

After lunch Sheriff Frank Atwood was recalled by the defense to go over his testimony regarding the Bartow County line. This was an attempt by the defense to have the case dismissed for jurisdiction. Atwood testified that the area where Patricia Ann Cook was murdered had always been commonly known as a part of Bartow County.

Mitchell used his cross-examination as an opportunity to further question the Sheriff about his conversations with Cochran during the trip from Fulton Tower. Atwood stated that he and Cochran had talked about Cochran purchasing a tractor-trailer and about Cochran's family and the fact that Atwood knew Cochran's brother.

MITCHELL: "Based upon those facts which you have just recited, and your observation of him, I will ask you to state, in your opinion, whether or not William Grady Cochran is sane or insane?"

ATWOOD: "In my opinion, I would say that he was sane."

ATWOOD: (In response to cross-examination by Corbitt) "No, I don't in any way hold myself out as an expert to tell the jury whether or not this man was actually sane or insane. My opinion on that would be just my best guess."

After Atwood's cross-examination, the defense rested.

The State re-called Dr. Thomas Peacock to the stand. Peacock again gave his education and credentials and stated that he was the Superintendent of Milledgeville State Hospital.

Upon questioning by Mitchell, he said that Willie Grady Cochran was released from Milledgeville on February 14, 1950, "as restored." He said that he was aware that prisoners sometimes feigned mental illness in order to be transferred to the state hospital. He said that Cochran was never diagnosed as schizophrenic in "his institution" and that the records showed that it was the opinion of the doctors at the staff meeting (when Cochran was released) that if Cochran had, indeed, been psychotic, it was due to the excessive use of Benzedrine taken while in prison.

In answer to questions by Mitchell, he said that he could not say that a patient could or could not be diagnosed after an hour examination and study of that patient's records but, he said, "In my opinion, as to what length of time would be the minimum in order to make a more accurate conclusion; well, the policy of the Hospital Board, which I determine, is that you have to have a minimum thirty days period of observation and study of a patient...sometimes we require longer, but we will not do it under thirty..."

Peacock was also questioned by the State about the diagnosis of paranoid schizophrenia. The doctor said that, in his opinion, persons suffering from this disorder, even if experiencing delusions and hallucinations, could be able to tell right from wrong.

Corbitt cross-examined the doctor for the defense. He questioned Peacock about the paranoid schizophrenic's ability to distinguish right from wrong.

PEACOCK: "If such a person...is living under a delusion or an hallucination, concerning certain outward manifestations, such as God telling him certain things to do, as to whether or not that person is always able to adhere to the right course, even though he might be able to recognize the difference in right and wrong; well not always. As to whether or not it is usual that this mental condition might cause him to follow what you and I would classify as a wrong, the wrong way, instead of the right, well, that might lead him to do so, but as I have frequently thought about these cases, if there was a policeman present they wouldn't do them."

Corbitt questioned Peacock about persons attempting to feign mental illness in order to avoid punishment. The defense attorney asked the doctor whom such a person might tell about his paranoia or other symptoms of mental illness. Peacock conceded that the person would most probably tell anyone who was observing him, and would likely tell "the prison authorities, the officers...well, in particular, anyone that might report to the officer in charge."

Dr. Peacock again stated that he had over eleven thousand patients in the state hospital, and he gave the qualifications of the doctors and psychiatrists there. He told about the general procedures of admitting patients, which included psychiatric examinations, chest x-rays, dental exams, blood tests and general physical exams.

PEACOCK: "With the shortage of doctors which I have down there...we attempt to give every patient that comes in some type of treatment, whatever is necessary, but we could give more psychopathia and more attention to patients if we had more doctors."

Corbitt asked whether or not someone thought to be faking mental illness would not have been released in less than seventeen months, especially since the institution would not want to waste limited resources.

Peacock would only state that Cochran was never diagnosed as paranoid schizophrenic, and that the record stated that "if he had ever been psychotic it was due to the excessive use of Benzedrine." He admitted that a Dr. Bradford (employed at Milledgeville) certified "that Grady was psychotic, that means insane."

Corbitt asked lengthy questions as to the method of diagnosing and treating schizophrenia, and the possibility of that condition not being correctly diagnosed. Dr. Peacock stated that was possible but not probable.

When Corbitt was finished with his questions, Mitchell conducted a re-direct examination and Corbitt conducted a re-cross examination. The basis of these questions was Dr.

Peacock's opinion of a mentally ill person's ability to tell right from wrong. He said that a person could know right from wrong and still "not be able to adhere to the right while suffering under his delusions."

It was just after three o'clock when Solicitor Erwin Mitchell rose to give his closing statement. Despite the afternoon heat, Mitchell faced the jury in his suit jacket and addressed them for almost an hour.

He advised the jury that the burden of proof, as to insanity, was on the defense and that Burdine's hour-long examination was not enough to prove it.

Pointing to the defendant, he challenged Cochran's statement that Patricia Ann Cook went with him willingly and suggested that she was forced.

In his conclusion, Mitchell retraced the crime and spoke of witness testimony. He reminded the jury that no conflicting statements were made by prosecution witnesses, and that no part of the testimony was denied by the defense.

Corbitt's final statement to the Court was brief. He said that Dr. Burdine could have been used again for the defense, but since Burdine had spent the better part of two days in court, he had been excused and released by defense counsel to attend to business.

The Court acknowledged Corbitt's statement and Judge Paschall charged the jury.

PASCHALL: "The defendant, William Grady Cochran, was indicted by the Grand Jury of this county at the present term of this Court, of the offense of murder. The indictment charges that he did, on the 20th day of June, Nineteen Hundred and Fifty-five, the County aforesaid,...then and there unlawfully and with force and arms, feloniously and with malice aforethought, kill and murder Patricia Ann Cook, by shooting her, the said Patricia Ann Cook, with a thirty-eight caliber English revolver, contrary to the laws of said place, and the good order, peace, and dignity thereof.

And to the charge...the defendant has entered his pleas of not guilty...you, gentlemen are to try and determine by your verdict."

Judge Paschall explained presumption of innocence and reasonable doubt. He explained that they were to make an honest effort to reconcile any apparent conflicts in evidence and to "believe that witness or those witnesses, whom you think are most entitled to credit at your hands." He went on to explain the definition of murder and how to determine if it had occurred.

As to the matter of confession he said, "It is for the jury to determine whether or not such alleged confession was in point made or not, and if the jury believe that there was a confession...a confession, alone, uncorroborated by other evidence will not justify a conviction. To make a confession admissible it must have been made freely and voluntarily, without being induced by another by the slightest hope of benefit or the remotest fear of injury."

If the jury should believe a confession was made but was induced or that hope was held out and/or there was fear of injury, "render a confession, if any inadmissible...the jury, in passing upon a confession or an incriminating admission, may if they see proper, accept a part thereof as true and reject a part as false."

Explaining the insanity issue he said, "A person shall be considered of sound mind who is neither an idiot, a lunatic, or afflicted by insanity, or who had arrived at the age of fourteen years, or before that age if the person knows the distinction between good and evil. A lunatic or insane person without lucid intervals shall not be found guilty of any crime or misdemeanor with which he may be charged, provided the act so charged as criminal was committed under the conditions of lunacy or insanity, but if a lunatic has lucid intervals of understanding he shall answer for what he does in those intervals as if he had no deficiency."

PASCHALL: "A perpetrator may be insane in a loose and general sense, and yet be, in the eyes of the law, sane and responsible so far as the act in question is concerned. This is a question of fact to be determined by this jury.

If you believe that the defendant committed the crime charged against him in this bill of indictment, but at the time of his confession he was mentally incapable of distinguishing between right and wrong...then you should acquit him. Likewise, if you have a reasonable doubt as to this, you would give the defendant the benefit of such a doubt. On the other hand, if you believed beyond a reasonable doubt that he committed this act, and at the time of doing so, if he did so, he did have sufficient mental capacity to know the difference between right and wrong, then it would be your duty to convict him."

The judge told the jury that if a person pled insanity, then it was upon that person to prove, by a preponderance of evidence, the plea of insanity.

Paschall charged the jury with bringing back one of four possible verdicts. If they found that the defendant did commit the act charged, the verdict would be, "We, the jury, find the defendant guilty."

He told them if they found him guilty, and saw fit to do so, they could go further and recommend mercy. If they chose that, the verdict would be, "We, the jury find the defendant guilty and recommend mercy."

The judge explained that if they found him guilty and went no further, his punishment would be death in the electric chair.

If they found him guilty and recommended mercy, he would be sentenced to life in the state penitentiary.

A third possible verdict would be, "We, the jury, find the defendant not guilty because of insanity."

If the jury did not believe beyond a reasonable doubt as to his guilt, they would bring back the fourth possible verdict of, "We the jury, find the defendant not guilty."

The jury left to begin deliberations at 4:38 p.m., and returned to the courtroom at 4:55 p.m. to hear a re-charge from Judge Paschall.

In his final instructions to the jury, Paschall quoted a Section in the Criminal Code of Georgia which stated that if a person were judged not guilty because of insanity, the judge would retain jurisdiction of the prisoner and order him to be confined in the state hospital. The prisoner/patient would not be released except upon compliance with the terms and provisions of another section of Georgia Law, under which other mental patients are discharged. This section states that patients of the state hospital "shall be admitted to, and discharged from, the Hospital under such rules and regulations as the Board of Control (of the Hospital) shall prescribe."

You Can't Play Outside...

Lastly, the judge charged the jury "that under no circumstances does the law say that...a general verdict of guilty...must be followed by the infliction of the death penalty. This jury is not limited or circumscribed in any respect whatever in your discretion as to whether you will recommend imprisonment for life in the penitentiary of the accused, Grady Cochran, if you find him guilty of murder.

It can never be said that the death penalty is demanded by the evidence after the crime of murder is established. If it is established, it is solely within the province of the jury whether the accused shall be recommended to the mercy of the Court. This discretion is not controlled by any rule of law and there is no criterion for the determination of a recommendation of mercy."

The jury retired to begin deliberations and to determine the guilt or innocence and the life or death of Willie Grady Cochran. They left the courtroom for the second time at 5:00 p.m. and returned with a verdict at 5:20 p.m., thirty-seven minutes since they first left the courtroom.

"We, the jury, find the defendant guilty," was their decision. No recommendation of mercy was made.

Judge Paschall called Willie Grady Cochran to stand before him as he passed sentence.

"The jury in this case has rendered a verdict of guilty for the offense of murder without a recommendation of mercy. It is therefore considered, ordered, sentenced and adjudged by this court, under provisions of law contained in the Code of Georgia, that the defendant, William Grady Cochran, be, by the Sheriff of Bartow County, Georgia, and such deputies as may be necessary, conveyed from this courtroom to the penal institution designated by the Director of Corrections of Georgia, and there held as provided by law, until the twenty-sixth day of August, 1955, and between the hours of eight o'clock a.m. and three o'clock p.m., on said date, be put to death by electrocution, as provided by law. May God have mercy on your soul."

Willie Grady Cochran's usually impassive face showed worry as he dropped his head. He had been subdued during the two-day trial, speaking only once or twice to his attorneys. He had not taken the stand in his own defense nor availed himself of his right to give an un-sworn statement.

After sentencing he was led from the courtroom without incident. He was rushed to a patrol car outside the courthouse and taken back to Fulton Tower in Atlanta.

Patricia's father and stepfather showed no emotion at the verdict. The courtroom spectators were told by the Judge to remain seated until Cochran had left the courthouse. Once he was gone the four hundred spectators left the building in a quiet and orderly fashion.

It had been twenty-five days since Patricia was murdered.

On the way back to Fulton Tower, Willie Grady suddenly began to laugh aloud. "That was fun wasn't it? Well, it's over and I got what I deserved."

CHAPTER 18

Soon after Cochran's conviction, his family hired an attorney from Atlanta, Paul Maxwell, to handle his appeal. He immediately filed for a new trial and was denied by Judge Paschall on October 6, 1955.

At that point, Maxwell filed an appeal to the Georgia Supreme Court. This appeal was argued before the Court on January 10, 1956, and decided on February 15th. Having lost that appeal, the attorney requested a rehearing, which was denied on February 29, 1956.

During that time, following his established pattern, Cochran made his last attempt at escape. Guards discovered partially sawed bars in his cell and transferred him to another section of the prison.

Cochran was brought back to Bartow County, under heavy guard, on March 6th, 1956, for his last re-sentencing. In a chamber session of Bartow Superior Court he once again faced Judge Paschall, and again he was scheduled to die in the electric chair. The sentence was to be carried out on April 13, 1956. He was calm and made no statement before or after sentencing.

As soon as it was over, he was taken back to Fulton Tower, where he remained until March 8th. On that date, he was taken to Georgia State Prison, then called Tattnall, to await execution.

Maxwell filed one more petition, this one to the Governor of Georgia, Marvin Griffin, for a sanity test. It was denied. This was approximately two weeks before the scheduled execution. Maxwell was quoted in the newspaper, at that time, as saying that there was only "one other thing" which might stop the execution, but he declined to say what that was. He also stated that he had not uncovered any other point of law that would warrant an appeal to the Federal Court.

With all appeals exhausted, Willie Grady Cochran's fate was sealed. The execution was scheduled to take place on Friday, April 13, 1956, between the hours of eight a.m. and three p.m.

While Willie Grady was at Fulton Tower, Jere White went to see him one last time. White was in Atlanta on business and thought to himself, "I think I'll go on over to Fulton Tower and see Willie Grady."

"It was a good day," White said. "You know Willie Grady had good days and bad days. On the bad days, he wouldn't talk much, but this was a good one and he was talkative."

According to White, in those days there was a lobby/visitation area on each floor of the Tower for attorneys and visitors to use. They were sitting in one of these areas and Cochran told him that he got what he deserved and that he knew that they could never let him, or people like him, out of prison. Cochran said that he knew he might do it again.

As they were talking, the elevator door opened and a jailer and an inmate stepped out. The inmate's neck was bandaged and his shirt was bloody from the neck to the waist.

White turned to Cochran and said, "My goodness, Willie Grady, something awful must have happened to him!"

Cochran looked at the inmate and said, "Oh, yeah. That's my cellmate. He has a death sentence, like me. He tried to kill himself this morning, cut his throat."

You Can't Play Outside...

White stated that Cochran related this information to him with absolutely no feeling whatsoever. It was obvious that Willie Grady was untouched by it and would never have mentioned the incident if White had not commented on it. White stated that it was apparent that human life meant nothing to Willie Grady Cochran.

On the morning of the day that Willie Grady Cochran was to pay for his crime, he had several visitors. His attorney Paul Maxwell had a short visit with him but left the prison, opting not to stay for the execution. Cochran's brothers and sisters visited that morning, but not his mother. Mrs. Cochran had been en route to the prison for a visit with him the day before he was put to death, but she had chest pains on the way and was taken back to Rome.

A reporter for the local Rome newspaper interviewed Cochran that morning and witnessed the execution. His account of their conversation appeared in the *Rome News Tribune*, but he never wrote about the actual execution.

The reporter spoke with Cochran at approximately 9:00 a.m. on April 13, 1956. According to his account, Cochran seemed relatively calm, but prison guards said that he had refused breakfast that morning. He spoke willingly with the reporter, but continued to maintain his silence as to the details of his crime.

When asked how he got the young girl to go with him, his response was, "I don't really know."

Asked if he had a final statement, Cochran replied, "All I've got to say is God bless my mother, my two sisters, sisters-in-law and brothers. God bless them all and everybody."

When questioned as to whether he had any message for Patricia's mother, he said, "Tell her if I've caused any trouble, I'm sorry. I've remembered her in my prayers. I've been forgiven of my sins and I'm at peace with God."

It was time. After days of being taunted by a young guard about the execution, Willie Grady Cochran calmly walked from his cell to the room that housed Georgia's electric chair. Several witnesses sat in the gallery. They included, among others, the reporter from the *Rome News Tribune*, Detective Bill Terhune, and at least one of Cochran's brothers.

Cochran showed no fear. He knew what to expect. During his previous incarceration at Reidsville, one of his jobs had been to prepare the bodies to be shipped home after execution.

The fatal shock was administered to Cochran at 10:15 that morning, and he was officially pronounced dead at 10:25, after spending eight minutes in the chair. His body was placed in a plain wooden box built at the prison and transported to Owen Funeral Home in Cartersville. This was the same funeral home where the body of Patricia Ann Cook was brought for autopsy.

Funeral services were held on Saturday in Paulding County at the Harmony Grove Methodist Church. According to the local paper "quite a number of floral offerings were sent to the funeral by relatives and friends." His cousin gave the family one of his own suits for Willie Grady's burial. His body was interred in the church cemetery and he was laid to rest beside his father.

Cochran was the last man, convicted of a capital crime in Bartow County, to be executed.

There was a monster inside Willie Grady Cochran. In order to destroy the monster, Willie Grady had to be destroyed.

You Can't Play Outside...

State Board of Corrections

Atlanta, Georgia

March 9, 1956

SPECIAL ATTENTION

Mr. R. P. Balkcom, Warden
Georgia State Prison
Reidsville, Georgia

            Re: William Grady Cochran
                  UNDER DEATH SENTENCE
                  Bartow Superior Court
                  Date of Electrocution: April 13, 1956

Dear Mr. Balkcom:

We are in receipt of a certified copy of sentence from the Superior Court of Bartow County, Cartersville, Georgia, which directs that the above named be electrocuted at the Georgia State Prison on the 13th day of April, 1956, between the hours of eight o'clock a.m. and three o'clock p.m.

You should therefore make the necessary arrangements to carry out the order of the court in this case, unless you are advised to the contrary prior to the above mentioned date.

Please immediately acknowledge the receipt of this letter.

                                  Yours very truly,

                                  STATE BOARD OF CORRECTIONS

                                  JACK M. FORRESTER, Director

JMF:cmc
cc: State Board of Pardons and Paroles
    cc: Mr. Wesley Smith, Clerk, Superior Court, Bartow County

Priscilla Sullins & Connie Baker

EPILOGUE

Our fascination with this crime began in our childhood, a place and time gone forever. It was a time of innocence and purity untouched by evil, and a place that exists only in our memories.

In that pivotal summer of 1955, we attained knowledge and lost innocence. We took a "bite of the apple" and recognized our vulnerability. Nothing was ever to be the same. Patricia Ann Cook and Willie Grady Cochran became our symbols of good and evil and, as such, were never forgotten.

Our research into this crime has answered many of our questions but raised new ones. There were also surprises. As children growing into adulthood, the case seemed to be all about Patricia Ann Cook. Once we began to put the story together we found that it was mostly about Willie Grady Cochran. Without a perpetrator, there is no victim.

Cochran certainly suffered from some form of mental illness and would, today, be termed a sociopath. It is undetermined to what degree he feigned or manipulated this disorder. There were times when he displayed a spark of humanity that evoked some feeling of compassion in those with whom he had contact, even those who researched his crimes. How much of this was manipulated and how much was real remains an unanswered question.

Cochran's criminal history includes two rapes and an attempted rape. Since even today many rapes go unreported, it's reasonable to assume that there may have been others. Was Cochran a serial rapist? Probably.

Cochran was convicted of murdering Patricia Ann Cook. He attempted to kill a cab driver during an armed robbery. Sources indicate he very nearly killed someone as a teenager and attempted to kill another inmate while in prison. These facts, coupled with his extensive travels in several states, fit the profile of a serial killer. Was Cochran a serial killer? Possibly.

Cochran was definitely guilty of the crime for which he was executed, and no one would argue with his statement, "Well, I got what I deserved." Yet, in today's courtrooms both the sanity hearing and the actual trial might have taken a very different turn. With less than ten months between the crime and the execution, 1950's justice was swift and certain.

This case also introduced two new laws into the Georgia Code. The fact that Cochran committed this heinous crime six months after his parole was a major issue. In the 1956 session of the Georgia Legislature, two bills were passed and signed into law by Governor Marvin Griffin.

Act 377 of 1956 created an advisory staff of technical experts for the State Board of Pardons and Parole. Experts in the fields of psychiatry and criminology were authorized to examine sex offenders and make recommendations as to parole eligibility. The law also provided that sex offenders could be committed to the state mental hospital upon completion of their prison sentence.

Act 457 of 1956 set up the first sex offender registry for the State.

Now, the children of the 1950's are middle aged and beyond. Most have married and many have children and careers, but Patricia Ann Cook will remain, in the words of sixties icon Bob Dylan, "Forever Young."

ACKNOWLEDGEMENTS

The writing of this book was a quest that we embarked on in January, 2001, but its inception was actually 1955, when we were children. To be a young girl in Rome, Georgia after the crime occurred meant being watched and warned about what could happen.

The horror of the crime and the names of Patricia Ann Cook and Grady Cochran were etched indelibly in our memories.

Our discussion of her brother's obituary brought to the fore many of those memories. We agreed that for both of us, this crime was a defining moment in our lives. Our innocence of the brutality that existed in the world was taken away forever. At ages eight and four we learned that all adults could not be trusted.

During this conversation, the idea to write a book was born. We knew that it would be a difficult, even daunting, task. After all, it had been forty-six years and we had full time jobs to consider. Time and availability of information were major factors, but we decided to make the effort.

Thus, the journey began. It was a journey that would take us to libraries, courthouses and through time, and we have many people to thank who helped us along the way.

At the outset we knew only that the crime had occurred in the fifties, so our research began locally, at Sara Hightower Regional Library. It has a Special Collections room with excellent resources and very helpful staff. There we were able to access newspaper articles on microfilm which gave us specific information to begin our research.

Equipped with names, dates, and places, our next step was a trip to the Bartow County Courthouse to research court records. There we were fortunate to encounter Melba Scoggins who is employed in the County Clerk's office.

Melba's assistance was invaluable. Not only did she aid us in accessing records, she also gave us the names of two men who were participants in the case, Judge Jere White and Mr. A. L. Woody.

On our second visit to the courthouse, Melba informed us that she had spoken with both men and that they were willing to be interviewed. She provided us with their telephone numbers so that we could set up appointments with them.

A special thanks to Melba.

Our first interview was with Mr. Woody. Meeting with him in his home, we had the opportunity to also speak with his wife. They are a charming couple, and both had recollections of the case to share. Those recollections and Mr. Woody's involvement as a deputy gave us a personal glimpse of the time and the man, Willie Grady Cochran. Thank you both for your time and your willingness to share your memories.

After setting up an appointment with Judge White, we met with him in his office at the courthouse. We spent over an hour talking with him, and his personal insights and knowledge of the case, and of Willie Grady, were very beneficial. A simple "thank you" does not seem enough to express our appreciation.

Our involvement with these three people in the early days of our research provided the impetus to continue our quest. Over the next year and a half, there would be others.

We would like to express our deep gratitude to those who gave us their time, knowledge, and memories. Without them and their encouragement, this book may have remained an idea. They include Sherry and Dallas Battle, Jim Burton, Robert Byars, Jonathan Cook, Herman Evans, Floyd County Police Department Chief Jim Free, Evelyn Hamilton, Callie Martin, Paul Polston and Jewell Studdard. Each of these people made a special contribution, some with their reminiscences, others with their referrals and introductions.

We were fortunate to have as our editors, a group of talented, competent, and knowledgeable friends. Their expertise was invaluable in the completion of this book. Heartfelt thanks to Don Black, June Bolt, Donna Freeman, Leslie Lucas, and Jan Whatley, and especially to Jeanie Cassity and Barbara Westbrook.

Friends who read our first draft and inspired us to continue include Stuart Honea, April Pugh, Brandi Starcher and Cathy Taff.

You Can't Play Outside...

Finally, we must express our sincere appreciation to our families. Our husbands, Tommy Sullins (with the red pen) and Ron Baker (with the never-empty coffee pot), always supported our efforts. Our children, Scott Covington, Whitney Sullins and Jacob Sullins, were patient and understanding of moms who were not always available.

ABOUT THE AUTHOR

Priscilla and Connie have been friends for twenty-five years. They were both born, raised and continue to live in Floyd County, Georgia.

Connie is married and has one son. She is employed at Rome/Floyd County 911. Priscilla is married and has a son and a daughter. She is employed at Floyd County Department of Family and Children Services.

This is their first book.

Made in the USA
Columbia, SC
25 November 2021